Look at My Striped Shirt!

The Phat Phree
Look at My Striped Shirt!
Confessions of the People You Love to Hate

Broadway Books
New York

PUBLISHED BY BROADWAY BOOKS

Copyright © 2006 by Phamily Business Entertainment

All Rights Reserved

Published in the United States by Broadway Books, an imprint of The Doubleday Broadway Publishing Group, a division of Random House, Inc., New York.
www.broadwaybooks.com

BROADWAY BOOKS and its logo, a letter B bisected on the diagonal, are trademarks of Random House, Inc.

Book design by Diane Hobbing of Snap-Haus Graphics

Library of Congress Cataloging-in-Publication Data

Look at my striped shirt! : confessions of the people you love to hate / Phat Phree.—1st ed.
    p.   cm.
  1. American wit and humor. I. Phat Phree.

PN6165.L66 2006
813'.608—dc22

                            2006043877

ISBN-13: 978-0-7679-2418-4
ISBN-10: 0-7679-2418-5

PRINTED IN THE UNITED STATES OF AMERICA

10 9 8 7 6 5 4 3

This book is dedicated to the soldiers on the battlefield fighting for everyone's inalienable right to be one of the assholes we make fun of in this book, to the entire staff at The Phat Phree who have the balls (or labia) to put their work out there every day, to the readers who let us know when we make them laugh, to the readers who let us know how much we suck and all of the suitably horrific ways in which we should kill ourselves, to the memory of John Ritter, and to the Quaker Steak & Lube all-you-can-eat Tuesdays.

Acknowledgments

When it comes to acknowledgments and thanks, no one does it better than old-school rap records. So that's how we're going to do it:

Special Thankz: Pat Da Taxman, Mrs. D, Beef, MGP Sr., Peggy P, The Rock & Roll Outlaw, Hummer Mike (Beder)—ride or die homie, Antifreeze T, Hawkman, Foley, JB the cornholer, the OG Crew: Z Man, Strictly Business JDL, Gracie, Emmett & da fam, SimOne, Papa Larry, Sleepy—swing lowe brother, MTL the font, **LCC & da crew:** Aaron McThug, Etters, the other dude, George G—where's my 40 at, dog?, LL Cool James **Da folks who made dis shit possible:** Big Byrd Leavell, Broadway Becky Cole, J-Sills, B-RamaJamma—sorry we are such a pain da ass **Much luv 2 da models:** T-Rex, Laaaara Ockaner, Meena K, Hadie from the block, Paul Dennis—get a last name playboy, Mad Mike (Fuller), Ryan Big Johnson, Clare D—they'll know your name now girl, Chris Klein—you iz way doper than the actor, Heather Macks, Eileen Lemish—git 2 it, Alisa with 2 last names, Dana Rader, B. George, Ross Ferrise—where you @, don't front on Mike Pfahl, Ted Achladis—you da man, Flyin Ryan Minnaugh, Chris Mead—sell those notebook player, Bad Boy Brett Sinning, the OG Striped Shirt Guy Nate Meers **Shout-outs 2 the peeps:** 2 the 216, 330 & 440, Big Pat—laugh it up, J-Clem from the 101 Crew, Sterile Ha, TMS, The Thought Nomad, White Gypsy, T Dubbs, the whole Compound Crew, Kung Lao, Funky Slice, The Trackside Squads—Fernando Peñis, Curfew "the Bible" Religion, Chris Rebel, Rusty Pitts, Snow Coleslaw Thomasson, Ted Diamond, DQ Denny Simes "the Blizzard," Cinnamon Stevensonton, Jesus Edwards, Dr. M.N.N.M. Gregory, Stitches, Jimmy Colo, Big Wil, Alx, Super Uncomfortable, Kool Moe Dee, Tucker, The Killa B's, Hugh "the Gentleman," Magic Zack, CAK, JG, KB and the K Crew, Falboo, RVV and CH Squad **2 Da Commenters:** Victor French, Christine, matt, deuce, Atlas, TomA, STEVE, HMK, Joe Kickass, Milton, Patrick, Don Bebe **Da Gas Face goes out 2:** all the haters—you can suck a warm dick, Steve Guttenberg, Terry Bradshaw **Mad Props 4:** all the people who make us laugh & anyone else we forgot. PEACE.

Contents

Contents

Contents

Preface

Look at our funny paperback book! Fucking read it! This book means one thing: We're going to be super famous!

Of course, once we are super-duper famous, we will all change. We'll start rooting for New York and Los Angeles sports teams. We will refuse to talk to anyone who is not at least as rich and famous as we are. We will join trendy religious groups. We will develop debilitating drug habits. We will date vacuous, gold-digging social climbers. We will start speaking out about politics despite the fact that we know nothing. And of course we will turn our backs on what got us here—namely, the raw, edgy, meaningful comedy that this book is comprised of, and the support of you, our loyal readers. Because being rich and famous is awesome, and we're not going to risk going back to being regular and broke by joking about hot-button topics or swearing. Just a heads-up.

But we're not rich and famous yet. So do your part to help us on our way toward the superficial and base existences that we so intensely desire by buying nine copies of this book. What will you do with nine copies of this hilarious book?

First off, read one copy of it, because it's fucking fantastic. I've never been given to hyperbole, but the writing in this book is so good that I think I can say that we make Hemingway look like a bush-league, two-bit faggoty hack. The Phat Phree staff painstakingly skewers the most depressing and most annoying members of this train wreck that we call a society in essays that are guaranteed to make you laugh, unless you actually are one of the douchebags that we are referencing, in which case you'll cry quietly to yourself while you comparison-shop handguns on eBay so you can end it all.

As for the other eight copies, two will make excellent his and her wedding gifts for that hard-to-shop-for couple. Four should be donated directly to your local elementary school, where they will undoubtedly be worked into the curriculum to better prepare our nation's youth for the world that awaits them. One should be buried in a plastic container in your backyard and dug up in two hundred years. I guarantee that by that point it will have quadrupled in value. If I'm wrong, I will provide a complete refund. The final book should take the hallowed place in your home of the guiding tome of your particular religion, whether it be the Bible, the Torah, the Koran, or *Maxim*. Whichever it is, you can just go ahead and throw it out. For in this book you will find all the spiritual comfort and metaphysical guidance that you will ever need, without all the boring "this guy begot this guy" talk and the constant threats of eternal damnation. Additionally, unlike the boring Bible, there are many hilarious illustrations of penises peppered throughout our book. Take that, Ecclesiastes!

Preface

So how 'bout it, chief? Pony up a few bones and buy a bunch of these bad boys. I figure we only need to sell about 50 million copies of this baby and we'll all be millionaires. And when that happens, you will no longer be of use to us and we can just go our separate ways.

Happy reading!

Chapter One

Who's Up for Going Out?

Look at My Striped Shirt!

Look at my button-down striped shirt! Fucking look at it! This shirt means one thing! I'm coming home with some pussy tonight! That's right! It's been a long week at the office, and it's time to blow off a little steam! I am a junior vice president! I have business cards that say "Junior Vice President" on them! They're glossy and magnificent! Here! Have one! Take it!

My boys are coming out with me tonight! They all have striped shirts too!

I figure we'll kick off the night with some Golden Tee! I am going to smack the shit out of that little white ball! It's going to be so fucking loud! I'll bet I can drive that pretend golf ball six hundred fucking yards tonight! I'm that fucking pumped!

I can almost taste those Jäger bombs right now! I fucking love Red Bull! I put it on my goddamned cereal! I'm crushing one right now!

I'm thinking about buying a boat this year!

I'm gonna fight someone tonight! I pray to God someone makes eye contact with me! I will beat his ass! And God help him if he gets any blood on my striped shirt! If he does, I'll scrub it out with his dick and some bleach! I mean it!

I'm gonna grind on girls' asses tonight! You heard me! When I see a group of girls dancing in a circle, I will select the most attractive one and dry-hump her until it hurts! I will rub my cock against her so that she can feel my throbbing hard-on!

I will valet tonight!

I will treat the valet with contempt and make sure that he knows that I am superior to him in life! I will tell him, "Take it easy on the brakes, champ"!

I will talk to people I don't know about my job tonight! They will all know that I am an important man! I will call female bartenders "babe" and male bartenders "chief"!

When I do not hook up with a girl at that club, I will say that the place is "full of skanks"! We will wait in a long line to go to another bar, only to strike out again!

I will give up and decide to order a gyro off a street vendor! I will make fun of him to my friends for being foreign! I will look ridiculous purchasing my gyro, because people will be able to tell by my striped shirt and tinted sunglasses that I struck out and am settling for a gyro!

I will make one last attempt to hook up by trying to coax two big girls who are also ordering gyros into coming back to my place for "after hours"! When they say no I will make fun of them for being fat! I will leave!

When I get home I will go to the bathroom and hold the straight razor to my wrist again! I will gently drag the razor laterally against my vein, making sure not to actually cut myself!

I will then go to my room and pass out! I will need some shut-eye so that I'll be ready to fucking party again tomorrow!

Striped Shirt Guy's
Top Five Red Bull Drinks

1. Red Bull and Jägermeister
Commonly known as the "Jäger Bomb," this is a true classic. When I want to party my fucking balls off till morning, this is where I turn.

2. Red Bull, Malibu, and Pineapple Juice
When I drink this it's like I'm relaxing on a beach or something, except I've got so much energy I want to fight a shark.

3. Red Bull and Bacardi 151
This is my emergency drink when I need to get messed up in a hurry. I usually bust this out on those rare occasions that I'm bringing home a "not-so-hottie." It eases the pain.

4. Michelob Ultra and Red Bull
I invented this drink and it's fucking money! I get the energy I need without all the carbs. These abs aren't going to stay this fucking perfect on their own.

5. Red Bull and Red Bull
That's right. Two Red Bulls at once. That's twice the energy! Just one of these cocktails and I could tear a fucking oak tree out of the ground. Fuck yeah!

I Am the Karaoke Master

Call my name! Call my fucking name, dude! I am READY!

"Debbie"? What do you mean, "Debbie"? That chick was just up there like two minutes ago, ruining a Shania Twain song. How the hell is it her turn again already?

I have more than twenty slips of paper up there with my name on them. Every song that I have selected is more perfect than the last. Just call me so that I can set this place on fire. My mad karaoke skills are gonna get me laid tonight.

Here's the plan:

First, I'm going to rock the house with AC/DC's "You Shook Me All Night Long." You know, to get the crowd on my side. I even do a hilarious Angus Young guitar solo pantomime right in the middle.

After that I'll slow it down a little and do something soulful to get the girls all lubed up. I believe some Creed might be in order. It feels like an "Arms Wide Open" night. I'll do a little intro describing how that Scott Stapp dude wrote the song for his son. That'll get 'em right off the bat. As soon as they see my pouty expression while I deliver that heartfelt, lyrical bullshit I might as well just throw on a condom to save time.

After that, it's time to show off the old sense of humor. If there's one thing I've learned, it's that chicks love dudes who crack their shit up. Luckily, I'm a certified cutup. I think I'll do Adam Sandler's "Piece of Shit Car." That song is fucking hysterical! The car he sings about is so shitty. Everybody will be rolling.

But wait . . . what if these morons really think I have a shitty car because that's what I'm singing about? That could backfire on me. Chicks hate broke dudes. Maybe I could say at the top of the song that I actually drive a 2002 Pontiac Grand Am. No, that would sound like I was bragging. It's not worth the risk, I'll just do a Weird Al song.

"My Bologna" it is.

By then, everyone will be sweating my mad karaoke skills, and that's when it's time to select a chick and do some duets.

First order of business: "Paradise by the Dashboard Light." They don't get any more classic than this one, and you can feel the sexual tension build throughout the whole goddamned thing. I wouldn't be surprised if she jumped my bones right in the middle of the baseball announcer part.

After that it's time for a ditty from a little musical called *Grease*. I believe "Summer Lovin'" is in order. Depending on my mood, I might even do the chick part and have her do the dude part just to score some extra laughs.

I'll play it by ear.

Then it'll be time to pull out the B-52's "Love Shack" and let nine bitches back me up while I do my patented Fred Schneider impression. I wonder if that queer had any idea when he recorded that song fifty years ago how much strange it would get me one day.

I'll wrap up the evening with my end-of-the-night showstopper, "Closing Time" by Semisonic. It's way appropriate because the song's called "Closing Time" and it's closing time at the bar. So it works on two levels.

After that, it's just a matter of watching all the broads duke it out over who gets to go home with the karaoke superstar. I hope it's that blonde over there.

Call my fucking name!

Does This Outfit Make Me Look Slutty Enough?

Girl One: I just bought the hottest outfit. It's so slutty! I am going to show thick cleavage and wear a mini and a thong that leaves nothing to the imagination. I will definitely yell at guys for saying sex-laced phrases to me, calling them "pigs" and "assholes" unless they are hot. In that case I'll smile!

Girl Two: Oh my God, girlfriend! That is awesome. I am going to drink Korbel and call it champagne before I go out just to get a buzz tonight.

Girl One: Hell yeah, chica! Let's sing songs we really hate incredibly loud even though the lyrics are demeaning to women. Honestly, do you really care?

Girl Two: Um, no! Women's libbers are granola crunchers! Let's do that ass dance that we do with a big group of girls while laughing as though it is funny!

Girl One: The club we are going to is so awesome! Have you been?

Girl Two: No.

Girl One: It's called "Lace." You know what it is . . . it's the same club we went to last year that sucked, but its new name makes it cool again!

Girl Two: Awesome! Let's wear our new slutty outfits so we don't have to stand in the line tonight. It gets so cold, and I am not even going to wear a jacket.

Girl One: Yes! Everyone will hate us because we will walk to the front of the line and get in because we're two single, anorexic-looking hot chicks with fake boobs.

Girl Two: . . . and don't forget—with phat extensions like Britney and Christina!

Girl One: I am so broke. Thank God I will not have to take my wallet out tonight! I am so hot that the men will spend their money on our drinks. I'll flirt and get them to buy them for you too.

Girl Two: I'll do the same, promise. We'll have to pretend we're interested in them and then say, "I have to go to the bathroom."

Girl One & Girl Two: . . . and never come back!

Girl Two: They will hate us when they see us talking to other guys!

Girl One: And then we pretend to never have met them!

Girl One: We have to be in VIP tonight. No matter how close the booth is to the others, we have to make sure there is a rope between us and everyone else, so that people know we are VIP.

Girl Two: That is so easy, chica—we just have to find the old foreign guys and make them give us drinks from the four-hundred-dollar bottle of Grey Goose they bought.

Girl One: They are so stupid! They always think we really like them. We should definitely dance on the booth and show guys how cool we are.

Girl One & Girl Two: We are so hot!

Girl One: I hope I meet a hot guy tonight who buys me fruity drinks so I can act more drunk than I am and have an excuse to kiss him and act slutty.

Girl Two: Totally! Then you can leave with him, make out in the cab, and go home and have sex with him—and he'll think you were just drunk! That will preserve your rep.

Girl One & Girl Two: We're going out!

I Don't Care for the Term "Door Guy"

What did you call me? No, say it. What the hell did you just call me? Yeah, that's what I thought. Listen up, loser: I don't like being called a "door guy." And if you say it again, I'll kick your ass to the curb.

I am night club security personnel. My duties are many, and they are important. My work is crucial to the effective operation of this establishment. And come hell or high water, I will have your respect.

A lot of people are under the misconception that my job consists merely of checking IDs, emptying garbage cans, and getting ice for behind the bar. And yes, I do all of those things. But I do so much more. I'm not getting paid seven bucks an hour just to sit on my ass.

I am a dress code enforcer. When some joker tries to sneak in here wearing jeans or tennis shoes, whose job is it to say, "No dice, dirtbag, head on back to the bowling alley"? That would be mine. If I weren't here, who would ensure that no one in this bar was wearing backwards hats, skullcaps, or do-rags?

In other words, who would keep the blacks out?

The bartenders? I think not. Those pretty boys and struggling actresses mix up drinks, not trouble. They'd be dead meat.

You need me.

I have this headset. It keeps me in constant communication with the manager and all my fellow security personnel. It's imperative that I tirelessly monitor my radio so that in the event of a violent situation arising I can be on the scene instantly. It's also convenient if they need me to bring some more Coors Light up from the basement cooler.

I catch about three fake IDs a night. My trusty U.S. state-by-state driver's license handbook never leaves my side. So if your birthday is in the wrong place on your Missouri ID, you can kiss that card good-bye, jerkoff. And don't try to get a fake military ID past me either, thinking I won't question it. I spent two years in the National Guard. God bless America.

We nightclub security personnel can smell trouble brewing from a mile away. Some people say that we overreact at times and get too violent. Nothing could be farther from the truth. For instance, on Techno Night last Thursday we saw these two little guys jawing at each other on the dance floor. Now, they hadn't actually gotten physical yet, but my fellow security personnel and I decided that the best way to defuse the situation was for four of us to jump on them and beat them into submission.

And I'll tell you what I told the cops: if you were there, you would have done the same thing. I didn't get into this business to make friends.

Of course, there are perks to the job. I get 15 percent off appetizers and all the soda I can drink. And let's just say that the chicks are big fans of the "Security" T-shirt. I guess it just emits a sense of authority that draws them to us.

But I don't have any time for that while I'm on the job. I don't like to mix my work with my personal life. As soon as I punch in, I'm all business. Because that's how it is for a professional.

Now if you'll excuse me, I just heard over my headset that someone puked in a urinal. I've gotta get on that.

A Brief History of the "Door Guy"

I Just Made Some Statements That I Can't Back Up

I'll have a Tanqueray and tonic. Thanks. Keep the change. Yeah, Todd, this bar is a little more crowded than I remember. With the game this afternoon, all the alumni—whoa! Are you okay, Todd? Here, grab my hand. Get you up off the ground . . . there you go. No, it was that asshole with the Ohio State jersey on. Not even looking where he was going, and he knocked you right over. Then he headed right out of the bar. Not your fault at all. Tell you what, if that asshole comes back in here, I'll kick his ass for you, okay? The least I can do for my old college roommate.

Of course, it wouldn't have happened if you had my sense of balance. My sensei has spent four years teaching me how to align my chakras. See? Look at my feet, hands, and head. Now, in the plane I'm in, it is impossible to attack me from any direction. I can see any threat to me with my fourth eye.

No, pineal gland is the third eye. Fourth eye is the gall bladder. I'm sorry, I can't tell you my sensei's name. He's wanted by the army of Myanmar, so he's got to remain incognito. Hell, I've been with him for four years and he won't even tell me what this secret discipline is named. Supposedly, when I've learned everything he knows, he commits suicide and I'm supposed to cook his gall bladder in a stew and eat it.

Check this out. This is called a death punch. If I used it against you it would instantly break all 206 bones in your body. The only other American who knew it was Bruce Lee, and he couldn't teach it to anyone. The CIA offered me forty thousand to show them how to use it against the Taliban, but I'd never break my oath. Although, if that jackass with the Ohio State jersey comes in, I might reconsider.

I can make nunchakus out of anything. Here, let me untie your shoelace. Okay . . . got it.

And I'll fold these two straws . . . like so! Looks harmless, right? But if I attached this spork, it would be illegal in seventy-one countries.

No, I can't teach you how you attach the spork. But I can show you this cool breathing technique. It allows you to delay orgasm for up to six hours. First, you—

What? Who came back in? Oh! Oh, no, I don't think it's the same guy who knocked you over.

That guy is much bigger.

No, my technique is really designed for people of roughly my same size. This guy, he outweighs me by at least a hundred pounds. Of muscle. And he's a foot taller, so the angles are all wrong.

Oh, no, no no, I know this other bar down the street that's . . . hey!

Hello! So. You're a Buckeyes fan, with the jersey?

Oh, you're on the actual team! Linebacker! Great! Screw Michigan!

No, sir, when my friend Todd said, "You're a faggot! My friend's gonna kick your ass with his death punch!" he was referring to another guy, who just left. Just a misunderstanding.

Quiet, Todd—I'll handle this!

Oh, hey, these must be your friends from the linebacking corps. Hello! May I have a moment to address everyone? Gentlemen, we are all gladiators, though we fight in different arenas. But the true warrior never fights in the arena of anger. No, it is the arena of self-discipline where his greatest battles are fought and won. So let's not focus on who called who a "faggot." Instead, let me buy each of you a Tanqueray and tonic and we'll drink to the spirit of our warrior ancestors, whom we'll honor today by fighting for peace. What do you say? No? Okay then, here, take my insurance card, Todd. And tell the doctors that I'm allergic to morphine. Now be a buddy and hand me that spork.

I COULD KILL YOU WITH...

I can kill a child or a woman with just six regular rubber bands. Three if they are sleeping.

I know it seems impossible, but a single feather has the tensile strength of three-inch steel pipe if you hold it at the proper angle.

You'd never suspect you were in mortal danger if I walked up with a handful of thumbtacks, but you'd be wrong—dead wrong.

Do you have a quarter? I can sever your spine with a quarter. Japanese coins are actually better for that.

I could kill everyone in this bar with a ham sandwich. What's so funny? I'm serious.

This Hot Chick Bartender Wants Me

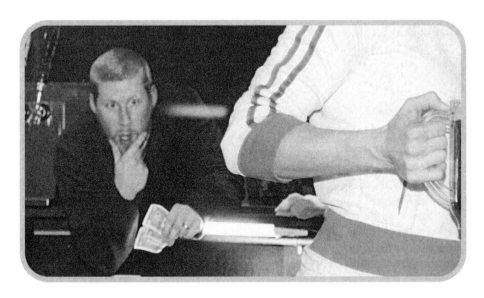

Good grief! Look at that barkeep. She is unbelievable! Look at that face. She looks like a cross between all the best elements of Catherine Bach and Salma Hayek. Jesus, she's an angel . . . And those cans, Christ am I a breast man. Those have to be at least full C's. Oh, man . . . she's coming this way—play it cool, play it cool. Give her the Barry White voice.

"Hi, handsome . . . What can I get for you?"

(in a low voice) "I'll have a Long Island."

"Okay, Long Island coming up."

Man, is she beautiful. There is no way on God's green earth that I could ever get a girl like that. She's amazing. I should probably just have one or two drinks and go home and masturbate.

After three Long Islands

Good God. I can't get enough of her. She probably has a man. He's the luckiest bastard since Billy Bob Thornton got to do that love scene with Halle Berry in *Monster's Ball*. Her stomach is perfect and her ass looks like two apples, one of which could have hit Sir Isaac Newton in the dome and caused him to pen the words to "Baby Got Back" instead of the law of physics. All right . . . here she comes again.

"You doin' okay, hon?"

(in an even lower voice) "Yeah, great . . . How 'bout you?"

"Fine, thanks . . . Can I bring you another?"

"Yep!"

I might as well just stick my leg in a wood chipper. It would definitely be less painful than knowing that I never have a chance at getting on that.

After six Long Islands

I don't want to jump to any conclusions, but I'm pretty sure she is checking me out. She keeps looking at me like every five seconds. I think she digs me. I think this could work! Maybe if I just keep drinking, throw her some nice tips, and keep the wit and charm coming strong, I can take her home. Here she comes . . . deep breaths. C'mon, man, you can do this.

"How's my favorite customer doing?"

(in a very, very low voice) "Great . . . how 'bout another LI?"

"Anything for you . . ."

"Hey, what's your name?"

"Courtney . . . what's yours?"

"Hans."

"Hans? Okay, Hans . . . Well, here's another Long Island for you."

What the fuck is the matter with me? Why did I tell her my name was Hans? I don't look German and I sure as hell can't pull off any accent. Dammit . . . I knew I shouldn't have watched that fuckin' *Die Hard* marathon. Watching that much TBS will fuck anyone up. You are my nemesis, Ted Turner!

After nine Long Islands

It is definitely on. She is into me; and that assertion is not in any way clouded by my epic consumption of alcohol. Tell me I have a condom. Who gives a shit, she looks clean. I'll hit that bareback. I'm going to rail her up against the wall like Patrick Swayze did that blonde in *Roadhouse*, and she's going to love it! Here she comes, play it cool. I can't let her know that I know that she knows what she wants to do to me.

"Hey, Courtney."

"Hey, Hans . . . another drink for you?"

"Yeah . . . You know what they say . . . never quit while you're ahead."

"Who says that?"

"Ummm, ahhh . . . you know, like the guys who say things. Yeah . . ."

"Ohhh-kay. Here's your drink."

After twelve Long Islands

Now seems like the perfect time to make my move. I hope she doesn't notice that I spilled those last two drinks on my pants and accidentally used the ladies' room the last time I got up.

"There she is . . . Courtney! There you are!"

"Hey, Hans."

"Who's Hans?"

"Do you need another one?"

"Um . . . so what are you doing after this? Partying? Or . . . 'cause, I party . . . hard . . . Ask anybody."

"Well, it will be about three A.M. when I get done here, so I'll probably just go to my boyfriend's house."

"What? Yeah, me too. I'll probably do that too. I mean, not go home to your boyfriend . . . Go home to my boyfriend . . . girlfriend, girlfriend! Go home to my . . . hot girlfriend . . . that I have . . . so I couldn't probably hang out with you anyhow . . . But, thanks anyway . . . Maybe some other . . . can I just cash out, then?"

"Sure. I'll grab your tab."

Well, that went better than it usually does. I almost had her. She has kind of a messed-up nose anyway. It's weird I didn't notice it before. That would be hard to deal with long term. Where's my jacket?

Hot Bartender Menu

I'm really sorry that you have no friends to talk to you and that no girls who aren't being paid to be here will pay attention to you, but if you insist on attempting conversation with me, please browse this helpful menu of the social pleasantries I am willing to give you accompanied by the amount of tips it will cost you.

A Thank-You..$1
And I hope you don't expect me to come back, you cheap prick.

A Smile..$2
Contrary to popular belief, two dollars does not mean you can call me "honey."

Hand-Touching...............................$5
I will BRIEFLY touch your hand while I take your money and smile.

Listening....................................$8
I will listen to one short story, but no sex stories, asshole.

An Assist..........................$10
I will laugh at one of your terrible jokes loud enough for another woman at the bar to hear me.

Free Drink.............$20
You get your next one on me—well, not me actually, it's on the owner.

Fake Number...$50
I will give you a fake number and pretend I would actually date you.

Real Number.....Market Price
Just keep tipping. I'll tell you when you've spent enough.

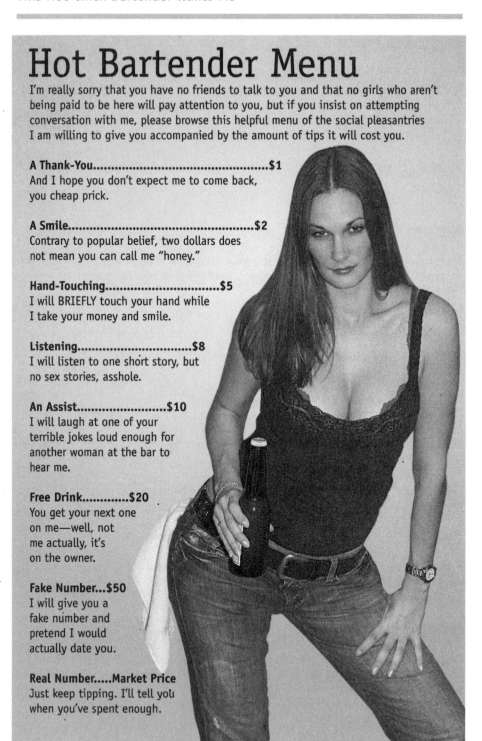

16

My After-Hours Party Is Going to Rock

Did you hear that, folks? Last call has officially been announced! Tick tick tick, everybody! McCarthy's Tavern is not going to be open much longer. These doors are gonna swing wide! But just because this place is closing doesn't mean you gots to go home. We can keep rockin' all night long. Everybody's invited to my place after this for a bad-ass after-hours party!

I don't want to get anybody too excited, but I very recently took up the acoustic guitar, and if I were a betting man I'd wager that you might all be treated to a little concert this evening. I can get through most of Green Day's "Boulevard of Broken Dreams." So there's one reason to come to my after-hours party right there.

I went ahead and purchased a case of Michelob Ultra off the bartender. He charged me sixty-five dollars, which is admittedly quite high. But these are bar prices. It's late. What are you going to do? I stand by my decision.

I took the liberty of personally inviting each and every girl in this bar over to my house directly following the closing of this establishment. Most of my invites were met with cold, derisive *no*s. Some ladies were feeling more playful and favored bitter sarcasm, assuring me that they would be over without a doubt. They then laughed with their friends as soon as I walked away. I pretended not to hear their scorn.

Some girls showed pity and gave feeble excuses as to why they weren't coming over in order to allow me to preserve some dignity. And for that I am grateful.

But the bottom line is, and let me be totally clear about this, there will be absolutely NO females at my after-hours party. And you can bet the farm on that shit. But that doesn't mean we can't have a good time. Right? Right.

Whenever I envision my after-hours parties in my mind, I like to picture a house full of people, tons of chicks (some topless), and everyone rockin' and rollin'. People are drinking and smoking herb. Everyone is complimenting me on my DJ skills. And then a goat goes running through my living room and everyone's like, "Where'd that goat come from? I guess anything goes at Dave Keel's after parties!"

And then, when the reverie reaches its climax, someone gets the crowd's attention and proposes a toast to me, Dave Keel, King of the After Parties. And everyone cheers and chants my name.

Well, this after-hours party won't be quite like that. In actuality it will be me and three of my dude friends watching *Old School* on DVD in my darkened living room again. We'll each open a beer that we have no desire to drink and take one sip out of it. When I wake up in the morning I will pour the other eleven and a half ounces of beer from each can into the sink.

See you guys there!

I'm Your Bartender, and I Hate You

I'm the bartender here, and that is an automatic license for me to hate you. So go ahead, assholes, tell me what you're having.

You want a top-shelf Long Island iced tea? I want you to know how much of an asshole you are for ordering a top-shelf Long Island. You put that much liquor in a glass and it could be paint thinner in there and you wouldn't taste the difference. But hey, it's your extra five bucks. If you don't spend it here, you'll just end up spending it on something else idiotic. Tell you what, I'm just going to go ahead and make you a rotgut Long Island and keep the extra five spot as my tip. See that plastic bottle of Kamchatka with the handles? That's all you, ass-munch.

All right, who was next?

You in the popped-up-collar polo shirt, what'll it be, hero? Five redheaded sluts? Oh, I see. You're going to try to get one of those girls drunk enough to sleep with you, huh? I'm not sure there's enough liquor in this bar for that. I tell you what, I'll save you the hangover and mix up a quarter ounce of alcohol with a quart of cranberry juice and watch all of you pretend to get wasted. That way at least you'll still be sober enough to rub one out when you get home alone. Thanks a lot—that will be twenty-six bucks, and don't forget the tip, Captain Hand Job!

It's pretty sad when the bartender is the coolest person in the bar by a HUGE margin. Next!

"Chief"? You motherfucker. I can't believe you just called me "chief." You're so lucky you ordered a bottled beer. If you ordered anything that I had to mix, I can guarantee that there would be some of my semen it in. I bring a Baggie full just for assholes like you.

No one in this bar deserves to continue living. Who's next?

Oh . . . Hey there, incredibly attractive girl who's obviously flirting with me in an attempt to get me to give her and her equally incredibly attractive friends free drinks. What are we having? What was that? Cosmopolitans? There's a shocker. So, what, I'm just supposed to comp these drinks because you're all hot? Do I look that pathetic? Well, you win this round. Here you go, beautiful. On me.

Who was next?

You three guys in the striped shirts. Let me guess . . . Red Bull and vodka? How did I know? I'm Jeane fucking Dixon, that's how. No problem, toolboxes; that will be $31.50, and you can't even have the rest of the Red Bull can, either. Just give me a twenty, a ten, and a five and walk away from my bar immediately. Don't say a fucking word to me because I will jump over this bar and kill you with my bare hands, you got it?

I can't wait to call last call fifteen minutes early. I own these losers.

What Your Drink Says About You

"I like it 'cause it tastes like candy and has bubbles!"
- Mimosa
- Sex on the beach
- Malibu and pineapple

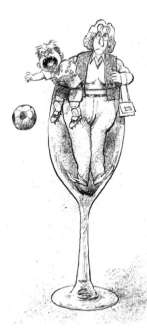

"Anything that will dull the screaming and help me forget about my unfulfilled potential."
- Boxed white wine
- Boxed red wine
- Bourbon and water

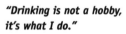

"Drinking is not a hobby, it's what I do."
- Dry martini
- Tom Collins
- Harvey Wallbanger

"I know two things: wine and loneliness."
- Pinot Noir
- Cabernet Sauvignon
- Riesling

"If it's in liquid form, I will drink it!"
- Keystone Light
- Moonshine crafted in frat-house bathtub
- Pledge brother's urine

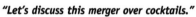

"Let's discuss this merger over cocktails."
- Scotch
- Brandy
- Port

We're Just Like *Sex and the City*!

Wait, I just realized something. Oh my God, you guys—we are JUST like the girls on *Sex and the City*! We're all single, successful, attractive women living in the Big City. Well, we might live in Kansas City—but it's still a city! We're basically just like Carrie Bradshaw and friends.

Okay, let me elaborate. Since I write *My Heart, This Land*, a regular advice column for the *KC Union Weekly,* I get to be Carrie. Also, we're both cute, wacky, self-absorbed man-haters. Plus, my column has a lot of rhetorical questions, metaphors about dating, and poorly developed theories about what men really want. Carrie loves having cosmopolitans at Suede, and I love having Smirnoff Ices at Pat McGuire's Pub and Grill. Same difference.

Janet, you're probably Miranda. I know she's a well-to-do lawyer and you're just an assistant at a law firm, but it's close enough. I mean, you DID finally pay off your Camry—that's pretty successful. Also, you're the most practical, momlike one who is overly neurotic and seems to hate fun. Also, she's kind of fugly and, no offense or anything, but we all know that you get laid the least. And your hair dye is reddish.

Jeanelle, you're DEFINITELY Samantha. Seeing as how you've banged every potent man in Kansas City that you're not related to, you are our own shining little beacon of female sexual empowerment. Remember, girl—next time you're lying there, in a cheap motel, you are not a slut. You are Samantha. Go, girl!

So that leaves you, Tricia. You would have to be Charlotte. It makes sense if you think about it—she's a prissy socialite desperate for a husband and children. You're a divorcée who blew her marriage settlement on painkillers and a Talbots account. Basically, the only difference is that you already have children—but since the court said you can't see them, it's kind of the same thing.

Just look at us, ladies—sitting here having brunch together, talking about boys and careers and relationships. Just like the girls on *Sex and the City*! Speaking of brunch, what are you guys gonna have?

I think I'm going to go with the Grand Slam Breakfast.

You Bet You Can Take My Order

"Go ahead whenever I'm ready"? Oh, you shouldn't have said that, my friend. By granting me the freedom to dictate when I will order, you're digging your own grave and the graves of the ten inexpensive-late-night-Mexican-food-loving drive-thru patrons in line behind me. I'm not going to be "ready" for quite some time.

I have no idea what I'm going to order. I am completely at a loss. This, despite the following facts:

A. I've already had more than enough time to look at the menu and figure out what I want while waiting in line for the past six minutes.

B. The overall item selection on your menu has remained essentially consistent for the past twenty years.

C. When it comes down to it, I always order the same thing anyways. Always.

Despite this, I'm going to have to ask you to "hold on one sec" while I foolishly attempt to do two things at once—read and breathe. Not my strong suit.

I'm going to talk to the people in my car for a little while now, if that's cool by you. They want to order stuff too but, much like me, have not even considered what they want until this very moment. "Hey, shut the fuck up back there! What do you guys want?" Sorry dude, these drunk sorostitutes are pretty loaded. We're probably the first group of indecisive, incoherent, intoxicated people to ever cruise through your drive-thru, aren't we? Oh man, we're hilarious.

You know what's not helping this whole situation? This sweet-ass speaker system you guys got. Seriously, where'd you get that thing, Gay-dio Shack? Up top! Kidding, bro. Hey, hold on one second.

(whispers . . .)Yeah, can I get some cheeseburgers, a milkshake, some vitamin D . . . (Honks horn, then screams) AWW SHIT! Had to turn up your headset?! Boo-yah! I bet your ears are bleeding more than a Sarah McLachlan concert at that time of the month. I'm the guy who started that. Seriously dude, back in '94.

Hey, what's taking so long; where's our food? Oh yeah, I haven't ordered yet.

Did I mention yet how loaded I am? I was higher than Richard Pryor tonight at this party. Afghani weed, bro. It made me feel all Arab and shit 'cuz I wanted to fuck, like, seventy-two virgins so bad.

You Bet You Can Take My Order

Hey, do you guys get benefits?

Bro, tonight I just wanted some T. Bell and some pussy, because T. Bell tastes like God candy when you're stoned! So does pussy, you know what I'm saying? What? I can't understand what you're saying, and I hate things I can't understand.

No, I won't turn my radio down. This is the new Hoobastank and there's only one way to listen to it: fuckin' loud.

My order's going to be huge. Get ready to work, Scooter, because I've got my sister's debit card. How much is a taco? That cheap? Yeah, I'll take two hundred of those fuckers.

Hold on a sec, shooting star . . . rad.

Hey, why are all the cars honking their horns? I already did that joke. "How about some originality, assholes?!"

Where were we? Oh yeah. Hey, do you sell pizza? No? Well you should. Pizza's awesome. Man, I want to go to France. Okay, I'll take a burrito, but can you make it all flat and just with cheese? What do you mean "that's a quesadilla"? Listen, man, I don't speak taco—just make it. No, you know what? Screw this and screw you. We're going to Denny's, where they appreciate our business! (*screech*)

Seriously, Dude, Give Me My Keys

All right, seriously, guys, ha-ha, joke's over. Now where the hell are my keys? And don't give me any bullshit about how you're just trying to be good friends. If you wanna be good friends, just give me my fucking keys so I can get the hell out of here.

I'm not even that drunk. I passed out leaning against that wall for like twenty minutes, so I'm good to go now. Power nap. And I told you I was sorry for throwing up in your aquarium. That was my bad. I fished the bigger stuff out with that little net. So how 'bout those keys?

This party is totally over, man, and I'm fiending for some Wendy's drive-thru, so let's do this. There are two junior bacon cheeseburgers and a five-piece nuggets calling me right now. Can't you guys hear them?

Look, for the last time, I'm fine. Dude, I'm fine. I told you, I stopped drinking whiskey like two hours ago. All I've drunk is beer since, like, midnight. Give me my keys.

Okay, this is not my keys. This is a pillow and a blanket. I'm gonna have a hard time starting my Dodge with a pillow and a blanket. I get it. You want me to stay here. And I would, man. For real. But I've got to get up early tomorrow. I'm supposed to go to brunch or some shit with my girlfriend's family. I've gotta be there by like ten or noon or something. I forget. Hold on, I'll call her.

Kelly! It's me. Where are you? What time's brunch tomorrow? Oh, that was today. My bad. Was it nice? Was there an omelet bar? What? I'm not yelling. You're yelling! Yeller. Hey, Kelly, they won't give me my keys. No, I'm fine. They're just being assholes. Here, tell them to give me my keys. No, tell them. No, I'm fine. I stopped drinking whiskey like four hours ago. Tell them to give me my keys. Why not? Why are you being such a bitch? Why aren't you ever on my side? I'm hanging up. Call me when you're off the rag. Wait, I love you. Hello? Kelly? Damn it.

All right, guys. I'm going to tell you something that I don't tell a lot of people, but you're kind of forcing my hand here. I know this is going to sound weird, but I drive better when I'm drunk. I'm serious. When I'm all fucked up it, like, really forces me to concentrate on the road. Ten and two the whole fucking way. I just turn on some old Rage Against the Machine to keep me awake and I'm good to go.

I'll make a deal with you. Can we all just be grown-ups here for a minute and make a deal? If I get tired on the way home, I promise that I'll just pull into somebody's driveway and take a nap.

What do you mean, "that's a terrible idea"?! I've done it before! You're a terrible idea!

I don't see what the big deal is. I have one of those "Friend of Police" bumper stickers on my tailgate, so you know they're not going to F with me. And I'll just use the back roads to get home. No, wait, I can't. It's all highway. But I'll stay out of the passing lane. I'll just chill behind a big old truck in the right lane, safe as a kitten.

No, I don't want coffee. That is of course unless my keys are in the coffee. That's the only way I'd want coffee. And that would be unlikely, not to mention unsanitary.

You know, I don't have to take this shit. I could just go out there and hot-wire my truck. I know how to do that. My buddy was a Navy SEAL. In fact, I think that's what I'll do. But I'll tell you this: you guys are paying to fix the damage I do to my dashboard. That's on you. All right, I'll see you guys later. Last chance to just give me my keys, save yourself a few bucks. No?

Okay, you called my bluff. I don't know how to hot-wire a car. My buddy Dave is a SEAL, though.

Fine! I'll stay here! Assholes! But I'm sleeping in your bed. You can sleep on the floor, Captain Lifesaver. And I can't promise you that I'm not going to wake up in the middle of the night severely disoriented by my strange surroundings and take a piss in your closet. It's happened before. Some fucking friends you are.

Ways to Avoid a DUI

Avoid highways as cops tend to monitor them closely. Try to stick to suburban back-yards.

If you see a parked cop car, immediately ram into it until it is no longer drivable. That's one less to worry about.

Pull over, shift into the passenger's seat. Tell cop your car's name is KITT and you have no idea why he was swerving.

When leaving the bar, cover your car completely with a huge piece of black fabric. What drunk driver? I don't see him.

Outrun them, you pussy.

Chapter Two

I've Got Some Stuff to Do

This Sunoco Is Now Open

All right, store's open! Queue up, you tooth-less fucks!

Just a reminder before we get started here: I am not one of you. I will never be one of you. This is a temporary job for me. I'm nine credit hours away from graduating and finding a nice comfortable job in middle management. My future's not what you would call bright, but it's not nearly as dim as what you all have to look forward to. All right, now who's first?

That's ten years' worth of Marlboro Miles you have there, dude. If I let you use all of them, you could take half the merchandise in this store and my fucking car. No, you cannot use all of them. This isn't the goddamned Depression. You get twenty. That's it. You're getting a free carton of smokes out of the deal, you greedy prick.

Jesus, man, must you actually shop for groceries in here? I know we're out in the sticks, but Christ, there's a Marc's about five miles from here—get your ass out there and stop getting raked. The bread's fucking four dollars, you poor dumb bastard, and there's six months' worth of dust on it. Someone should fly Ted Kennedy out here so he can see that poor people aren't poor because they're getting fucked over by Republicans; they're poor because they're jagoffs who buy groceries at the gas station.

Yes, those EZ Widers are a buck forty-nine. No, the price is not "Jewish." I am Jewish. The price is not. I did not make the price. The owner of this establishment is a Bible-beater. Maybe you should tell him the prices on rolling papers are "Jewish." I have no interest in hearing your bullshit, but I will, because if I tried to raise up you guys would take me out back and hang me by a fucking tree or something. You want free papers? Fine. Take them and get the fuck out of here. Don't steal anything on the way out, you filthy redneck.

Hey-hey! Nice ground effects, champ! Say, you do know *The Chronic* came out a fucking decade ago, don't you? Hey, man, there's this awesome new group I just heard. They're called the Fugees. You should get into them, Nineties Boy—they're hot right now. If you're going to be a fucking wigger, at least be reasonably up to date.

Let me guess, ma'am—pack of Basic Lights? I knew it. How far along are you, hon? I won't ask, because if I vocalized your pregnancy it would make me so sick that I might smack you across your face with this hard pack. Oh, I shouldn't talk because I'm a man and I don't understand. Maybe I don't. What I do understand is that you're a retard, and if they ever figured out a way to abort the mother and not the baby, I'd be pro-choice in a New York minute. Yeah, yeah, here are your smokes. Good luck with that little Ted Bundy you're gestating right now. Real promising future for that kid. Look out, Harvard.

Jesus Christ. You again? Four dollars on pump four, huh? Hey, you know, you put four dollars in that Dakota of yours yesterday . . . and the day before that . . . and the day before that. Why don't you just fill it up, you cheap fuck, so you don't have to come in here every day and bother me while I try to read the sports page?

All right, store's closing. And don't anyone dare to drive up to the pump while I'm shutting off the lights and setting the alarm. I'll kill your entire family.

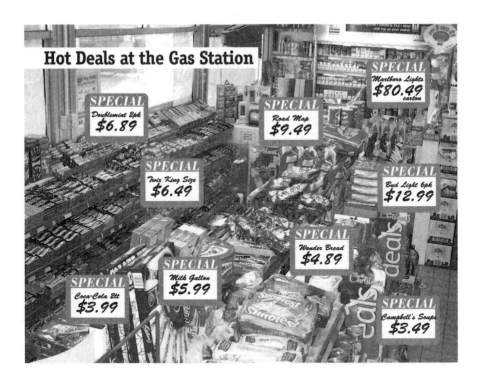

I'm Your Cool Teacher

Gooood morning, everyone. Welcome to geometry class. I'm your teacher, Mr. James. But you guys can call me Tom, or T, or T-Bone, or whatever. Let's not get all hung up on labels. I don't want you guys to think of me as just another square teacher. I want to be much more than that to you. Partly because I've never been a big fan of the conventional student/teacher relationship, but mostly because I'm insecure and lonely and am therefore utterly desperate for your approval.

So I recognize some faces out there. Particularly those of you who play sports. Go Tomahawks! However, you're going to have to be patient with me as I learn your names if you don't play a sport or if you're on the soccer team.

Let me tell you a little bit about myself. I wear tight blue jeans to work, as I find this further breaks down the barrier between student and teacher. Just because I'm a teacher doesn't mean I can't dress cool. As you can all see, these are button-fly. I complement the Levi's with a sport coat in order to appease the powers that be, but if you guys ever see me outside a school setting (which I am completely open to—anybody here Rollerblade?), you'll see that when I'm on "my time" it's a T-shirt and jeans or nothing for me. In fact, I've got my Goo Goo Dolls tour T-shirt on underneath this little ensemble right now, and she's ready to make her appearance come about three o'clock. Anyone else here down with the Dolls? No? Me either, really. I'm just wearing it as a goof.

If you're worried about this class, don't be. I assure you, ALL of you will get A's with little to no effort, and you won't learn a thing. For the first twenty minutes of class you'll probably ask me a bunch of silly questions that lead me away from the topic that day. I'll fall for it because I'm desperate to share details about my life and make a connection with you. You will act as a collective therapist to me as I drone on about my personal life. If listening to me talk about my marriage makes you happy, then boy howdy, have you hit the scholastic jackpot! I'm divorced with two kids your age, so you're in good hands. The whole lot of them hates me with the white-hot intensity of a thousand suns. I just bought a sweet Trans-Am with the money I should be paying for child support. Shhh. I trust you.

When I finally get into the lesson I'll blow through the chapter in about ten minutes, leaving you the remainder of class to "read quietly," which just means do whatever the hell you want.

Here are some things I allow in my class that other teachers don't: eating, drinking, swearing, dancing, smoking, spitting, praying, fighting, cell phones, headphones, Texas hold 'em, camera phones, microphones, iPods, and sex. But just oral—this isn't a free-for-all.

As a matter of fact, the only thing I don't allow in my class is for you to not like me. But if you find yourself not liking me, then please just let me know and I'll make whatever adjustments are necessary to change that.

I have a field trip to a brewery scheduled for no reason. Which reminds me, if you guys get in a pinch, I am available for beer runs regardless of the time of day or night.

Do you like Nelly? I love Nelly. Unless you don't. Do you?

I'm very, very, very liberal. I'm so liberal, I'm from Liberia. I tell bad jokes like that because I'm out of touch and can't help it.

This is your class, not mine. In fact, you're smart kids. You don't need me here. I'm going to leave. Have a good year and I'll see you at all the sporting events! If you see me there, please come up and talk to me.

Mr. James's Final Exam

1. This triangle is
    a. obtuse. (nope)
    b. four-sided. (LOL)
    c. acute. (It's this one, gang.)

2. Area can be measured by multiplying length and
    a. boring.
    b. who cares?
    c. width. (Ding ding ding!)

3. What was your favorite day in Mr. James's class?
    a. The day we watched *Boogie Nights*.
    b. The day Mr. James brought in his guitar.
    c. Every day—duh!

4. Where is the party at this weekend?
    a. Kevin's house.
    b. Jessica's house.
    c. Mr. James's crib. (I've got wine coolers!)

5. (A ladies-only question) I think Mr. James looks best in
    a. his olive-green American Eagle sweater.
    b. his Tupac *All Eyez On Me* concert T.
    c. anything!

Have a rad summer, gang! And please sign my yearbook on the way out.

Seriously, Get This Sweater Off Me

I mean it—I feel ridiculous. Get it off.

Lady, just because your boyfriend doesn't want to settle down doesn't mean you should pretend that I'm a real baby in hopes that he'll play along in your twisted game of house. You're scaring him off, and it makes you look insane. You dress me like a Gap employee and tote me around like a fashion accessory. It's disgusting, and you need to get your shit straight. Meantime, you can stop force-feeding me Altoids.

While I'm on the record, there are some other things I could do without. Yeah, as it turns out, I don't really care for the ylang ylang oil massage. It's not relaxing. It actually hurts and generally creeps me out.

Oh, this just in, I'm not actually a fucking vegetarian. Do you honestly think that I prefer couscous and tofu to my lamb and beef nuggets? Lettuce wraps? Are you serious? What is your damage? I would rather eat my own shit, and guess what, when you're asleep, I do. Then I lick your face and laugh about it.

Don't even get me started on my name. Louis Vuitton? Do you have any idea how embarrassing that is? I'm already wearing the gayest sweater since *The Cosby Show*, but you insist on naming me after an expensive line of European handbags. Seriously, fuck you. You make me look like a complete pussy, and I hate you for it. For real, the next time you try to gel my hair, I will tear a hole in your windpipe. I swear to God I will.

Not that you'd ever fucking notice, but you continue to place me in dangerous situations.

Just yesterday at the dog park, I could feel the cold hard stare from a Doberman through my Kenneth Cole double-breasted peacoat. Shit, even the French poodle called me a fag, and he was wearing a beret.

Do you have any idea what would happen to a dog like me at the pound? You don't even WANT to know. I step in there with even a whiff of CK One on me, and it's all over.

It pisses me off that you don't pull this shit with the cat. I am really tired of the smug looks I get from that butch-ass feline. Just once I'd like to see you put an ascot around her neck and let her feel what this shit is like. Then she'll realize it's not funny and I'm in real pain here. I promise I will end all nine of her lives if I ever get a chance to chase her without these miniature Steve Madden patent leather urban utility boots strapped on my paws. Not that I'd get far; even without the shoes I still have to battle these Italian microsuede chinos.

And just for the record, I don't need friends. I'm a dog. The whole concept of Dogster is ridiculous. There is nothing more humiliating than being held up to your Web cam and forced to wave at a Pomeranian in Lansing, Michigan. This is about your need for contact with the outside world, not mine. Just because you're socially retarded and can't make friends without the use of Web sites doesn't mean you have to drag me into it.

Listen, lady, I'm at the end of my rope and I've been doing a lot of thinking, because there's a lot of time for that while you watch E! and thumb through your copy of *People* magazine, stopping occasionally to read the text message on your jewel-encrusted Sidekick. I have decided that I'm running away. I'm going to take my chances on the outside. Tomorrow morning, during doggie yoga, I am fucking gone, baby.

It's Ladybugs for Me!

I have loved ladybugs ever since I was a little girl. It's funny, because you never think of bugs as being cute, but with their red little wings with tiny black spots, I find them absolutely adorable.

I began collecting ladybug knickknacks about ten years ago, and over time my collection has become enormous! It's at the point now where you can't walk into a room in my house without being reminded that I am just cuckoo about ladybugs!

I have ladybug salt and pepper shakers, a pair of ladybug throw pillows, ladybug bedroom slippers, and even a ladybug-shaped telephone! The other day when I was at Jo-Ann Fabrics, the cashier, Kelly (who knows I'm a certifiable ladybug nut), showed me some new fabric with ladybugs on it that they had just gotten in. I purchased two yards of it and made a neckerchief for our Yorkshire terrier, LadyBug. When I was tying it around his neck he glared at me as if he were thinking, *When is someone going to end her pitiful and empty life?* I don't know, LadyBug—your guess is as good as mine!

Some people are very difficult to purchase gifts for because they are somewhat psychologically complicated and their lives are multifaceted. But not me. Everyone knows that all you have to do is get me something with a ladybug on it and I'll light up like a retarded kid at a pro wrestling match! Last Christmas alone I was given a pair of ladybug earrings, a cute ladybug apron, and some lovely stationery with, you guessed it, ladybugs on it! And I couldn't have been happier.

Ever since my son and daughter moved out and my husband started having an affair with a fellow worker at his Century 21 Realty office, I've just had that much more time to browse the Internet looking for interesting new ladybug items to add to my collection. I currently have an eighteen-dollar eBay bid in on a ladybug-shaped dessert tray. I hope my bid holds, but truth be told, I'd probably go as high as thirty-five dollars.

Sometimes I think to myself, *Diane, what would be the most fitting way for someone to do society a favor and end your life?* And I think I've finally figured it out. I would tie me up and force-feed me thousands of live ladybugs. Then I'd duct-tape my mouth shut. During those few fleeting moments before death claimed its prize, I believe that even someone like myself could not help but recognize the powerful irony of the fact that I was suffocating and choking on the very thing to which I had dedicated my vacuous life.

And then it would all go blissfully dark.

Being a Cop Makes Me Important

Afternoon there, Cochise. You're probably wondering why I pulled you over, aren't you? Yeah, that's understandable. Well, lemme give you the 411. It's a little violation called "speedin'." And I'm not having it. Not on my watch, Jeff Gordon. I clocked you at thirty-nine MPHs. The speed limit through here is thirty-five. Now, four MPHs might not seem like a big deal to you, but it's a slippery slope. I let ya get away with four this time, and next time you'll tear ass through here at six over. It's a vicious cycle.

I take my job seriously. A little too seriously, according to many people I know, and I tend to agree with them. But don't blame me. Blame the traumatic childhood experiences I endured growing up. For that is truly what turned me into the bitter, vindictive prick cop that now stands before you.

Adolescence is such an awkward period in our lives. And as an overweight youth with poor social skills, I sustained physical and mental mistreatment during those important formative years that had dramatic effects on my character and self-image.

And while I'm no psychologist, I would imagine that having an abusive, drunken stepfather as the primary male figure in my life contributed greatly to my nasty nature, not to mention my disrespect for and objectification of women.

Regrettably, I always lacked the intelligence and people skills to obtain authority by admirable methods like hard work, personality, and a college education. But I still craved the ability to intimidate people and force them to respect me. That's where the police academy came in handy.

After just two months at that fine institution I was somehow able to garner the ability to torment people of all levels of intelligence and class, even those that far exceed my own. Whether you're a prissy college boy, a Nobel laureate, or even one of the two senators that represent this fine state, you are my bitch. I can detain you, patronizingly question you, or force you to do the DUI agility tests just for my own sick amusement, even if I am secretly certain that you haven't had a drop. God bless America.

Okay, with that being said, I'm going to need you to go ahead and step out of your Lexus there, because that is a nicer car than I will ever be able to afford, so

I'm afraid I'm going to have to hassle you for a bit just to set my mind at ease. During this procedure, I'll be blatantly leering at your wife, who is far more attractive than my own and is therefore also subject to my contempt. So if you could just go ahead and put your hands on the car and spread your legs, that would be great. And I assure you that this will be as uncomfortable as I can possibly make it.

To Serve and Protect

High School Bully
This guy got into police work for one reason and one reason only: to legally beat some ass. Pity the jaywalker within his reach if this cop had a fight with his wife last night or lost fifty bucks on the Knicks game. Someone has to pay.

Mall Security Guard
This variety of cop is composed primarily of disgraced ex–police officers and men who were actually too dumb to join a real force, and that's saying a lot. His beat, which usually extends from the food court Sbarro to Spencer Gifts, is patrolled halfheartedly as he keeps an ever-watchful eye out for Suncoast shoplifters and rowdy teens who are misusing the escalator.

Poser PI

This cop saw too many action movies in which police did cool things like unravel international espionage attempts and stage undercover drug busts. He wishes that his job were composed of such action. Sadly, not only was he on school crossing guard detail this week, but he also had to climb a telephone pole to pull down a dead cat that some kids threw up there for fun.

Officer Good & Plenty

Sure, he passed his physical—thirty-five years ago. Since then, he may have lost some of that pep in his step, but rest assured, while this cop is on the job no late-night deli, pie-serving coffee shop, or White Castle drive-thru is left unpatrolled.

No Substitutions, Y'all

Let's get this straight: we can't do substitutions. I've worked at this Hooters for more than two years, y'all, and my manager, Rebekah, always says no. I stopped asking her after I got trained. We got calendars for twenty-five dollars, we got shirts, and we got what's on the menu. That's it. God.

We ain't got snapper. I'm tellin' y'all. Anyways, I don't know what's so funny about it. Our fish is a grouper fillet sandwich fried golden brown and served with tartar sauce. It goes great with a pitcher of Bud Light and a calendar. But, no, snapper is not on the menu, so will you guys please quit askin'?

Sorry, guys, you can't get a fish taco. They sound good to me too, but we don't got 'em. Maybe I should talk to Chad, the owner, when he comes in. I mean, Tallahassee has some good seafood places—maybe it's time Hooters took a fresh look at its menu. For how many times y'all order 'em, I bet they'd sell faster than our "Nearly World Famous" wings!

I had a group of guys in the other day. They came in to watch the race. I was totally nice to them. I sat down and introduced myself. I said, "What are y'all up to today?" I thought they liked me. When they left, I even gave this cute guy my cell number. But when I was cleaning off their table, I found one of them comment cards. One of the guys wrote they were never coming back here because we don't serve bearded clam. I could get in trouble for that, guys. Chad is always readin' those cards, and it's not my fault—I don't choose what to put on the menu. I'm just trying to work my way up to floor manager. That way I can wear a shirt with sleeves. *We got clam chowder. Isn't that good enough?*

It's hard enough working here with all the creepy guys that come in. I mean, you guys seem cool, but can you just order something that's on the menu? If I could go into the kitchen and make you a side order of beef curtains, I would.

Hooters' seafood selection might not be that great, but I know we got a great burger menu. I've never had a fur burger before, but we have a mushroom and swiss burger you might like. It's pretty good, and it comes with fries too. Can't you guys just stick to the menu?

And what's with all these questions about the roast beef? It's slow cooked and served with a side of au jus. Who cares how low it hangs? I don't even know what that means.

And can y'all stop drawing pictures of penises on your credit card receipts? Thanks.

Buy Something at My Shitty Garage Sale

Hey, buddy. I see you're checking out those Cool Whip containers, huh? You've got a good eye, my friend. You weren't? Well, that's too bad. A fella could keep pretty much anything he wants in those. It's just like Tupperware, really. Same thing. But that's cool. It's your loss. Just keep looking. I'm sure you'll find something you want to buy at my shitty garage sale.

Looking to update the old wardrobe a bit? Well, you came to the right place, my friend.

How about this long-sleeved shirt that has the word "Aeropostale" really big on it? This was a gift from my mom. I've never even worn it. What a great way to look fashionable while letting everyone know that you shop at Aeropostale! Not your style? I hear you.

Well then, how about this Darius Miles Cleveland Cavaliers jersey? At three bucks, that's a steal! He's doing some great stuff in Portland nowadays. No, it's not "dated." It's a "throwback." That's the look right now. It's what all those rappers are wearing.

Come on, dude, buy something.

How about this Nintendo entertainment system? This thing's a classic! I'll even throw in a couple of games. Say, the "Bad Dudes" and "Super Mario/Duck Hunt" combo. Five minutes of playing those and you'll say, "Xbox what?" Yeah, the door part broke off the console a long time ago. But it still works if you blow in it a little. No, I don't know where the little gray box–TV connector piece is. But you can get one of those at any Radio Shack.

You a movie buff? I've got some great VHS tapes over here, and it's just killing me to part with them. Remember *The Mask*? Jim Carrey was so great in that! With all those crazy faces he makes. Or how about *Father of the Bride 2*? Steve Martin's back and his family's still driving him nuts! Gonna pass on that? All right. It's your funeral, man.

How about this Ab Roller? This was endorsed by that ponytail guy. Summer's right around the corner, man—are you ready for swimsuit season?

Buy Something at My Shitty Garage Sale

Buy my sociology textbook from college! The bookstore wouldn't buy it back because they weren't teaching this class the next semester. You should buy it. What do you mean, "no, thanks"? I guess you know everything there is to know about sociology, huh professor? My bad. I wasn't aware of that.

Well, there has to be something here at my shitty garage sale that you want to buy.

One TV tray?

A Sit 'n' Spin?

McDonald's Christmas glassware?

Most of a tent?

Word processor?

Key Bank T-shirt?

Michael Crichton *Jurassic Park* paperback?

Lamp with no shade?

Nelson "After the Rain" cassingle?

Rotary phone?

Come on, dude. Buy something. Jesus.

I'm Going to Hook You Up with This Cell Phone, Bro

Hey, my man. Can I help you? Lookin' for a new cell phone, huh? Yeah, well, I'm sorry, but we don't have any phones here.

. . . I'm just messing with you. Of course we have phones. In fact, all we have are phones—well, phones and phone accessories. What are you looking for? Something inexpensive? Whoa, hit the brakes there, Penny Saver. Are you married? Girlfriend? Ah, single! Me too, bro. Why stick with one box of cereal when you can get the variety pack, right?

Stop right there—I think I know what you need. Have you heard of the Treo 650 smartphone? Come over here and take a look at this. It's got a three-inch screen, built-in PDA, camcorder, e-mail, video, Internet access—

You just want to make phone calls. Phone calls to who? Ladies? Listen, pal, if you are looking to get your wick wet, you can't be afraid to shell out the cheese on a bona fide babe bagger like the Treo 650. I mean, if you were going out deer hunting, would you take an air pistol or shotgun? A shotgun, am I right?

You're GD right I'm right. This is the double-aught-six of mobile technology. This baby will land you a trophy that you can mount on your wall . . . and your floor . . . and the backseat of your car . . . You know what I'm saying? HA!

Can I be frank with you? I bought this phone six months ago, and I have gotten more USDA Grade-A trim than ever before. You flash this baby at the club and you will ruin a lot of panties. You hear me? Moisture . . . in the vagina.

Let me ask you a question. You ever had two women at the same time? Because I have to tell you, since I've had this phone, I'm sick of them. Seriously, it seems great when you hear about it, all the extra boobs and the wild moves. But it's exhausting. I pray for just one night when I am not trying to satisfy two hot mamas. But there are worse problems to have. Am I right?

See, you get it. Listen, I like you. If you buy the Treo and the Bluetooth wireless headset, I can give it to you for $429. Nobody else gets this deal. I can't let you walk outta here without the headset. The headset is the key to Labia City—

I'm Going to Hook You Up with This Cell Phone, Bro

Strictly business. I like that about you. You know, I never do this, but do you wanna go out to the clubs with me tonight?

Oh, come on. It's cool. I'm just going to go ahead and put your number in my phone so that I can give you a call. Word? No?

Okay, okay. That's fine. I just wanted to . . . you know, hang with you. You've got the Treo 650. I just figured maybe we'd have some luck if we went out together. You know, tag-team. Maybe we'd score some ladies who were down for it—way down. Right?

Okay, can I be honest here for a minute, bro? That stuff about being sick of the threesome, that's not true. I really need to get laid, and I think a cool dude like you could make that happen. You've got that cool phone and all that.

Ohhh, I see . . . you got a Treo 650, so I am not good enough for you. You know what? You have really changed, man. I mean, now you have this awesome phone, and it's like we were never friends.

Don't play dumb. I see how you're looking at me.

You know what? Fuck you. I made you. I fucking made you. If it weren't for me, you'd be walking outta here with a fucking LG. Now get the hell outta my store! And don't call me! I will call you when I feel like it! And no sooner!

I Have a Request, Mr. DJ

Am I on? I am? Yeah, I'll turn down my radio. Hold on. There we go. Anyways, I have a request.

I "request" that you never play "Mississippi Queen" by Mountain again.

Do you honestly think there are legions of listeners out there that pump their fists every time that opening riff comes on and say in unison, "Yes! I fucking love 'Mississippi Queen'!" Who do you think you're pleasing by playing that nine-hundred-year-old song, which was shitty when it came out, over, and over, and over again?

See, I work second shift at this factory. I put together brake parts for semi trucks. It's bad enough that I have to wear safety goggles and stand on a concrete floor for eight hours while surrounded by people of a lower station than I, but I can take that. I can take it that there are no women here who I'd rather fuck more than the palm of my hand. I can take that it's hot, and that putting together brake parts involves a monumental amount of repetitive stupid-work. It pays for my beer and bammer, so I'll do it. But you know what really chaps my ass? The factory radio is always tuned to your station. And every night, twice per night, you come on the air with your smug voice and rasp into your microphone: "All right, comin' out to Dawn in Westlake, here's some 'Mississippi Queen' " or "And now Fairview Park is rockin' with Mountain—here's a little 'Mississippi Queen.' "

You're a lying sack of shit. Nobody out there is really calling you up, requesting "Mississippi fucking Queen." Not Dawn in Westlake, not the guys down at B&J Auto Sales—nobody. I simply can't believe that. And if those people really are out there, well . . . you might only be the beginning of my rampage. Because as far as I'm concerned, anyone who will call a radio station to request "Mississippi Queen" doesn't deserve to live.

I'm not fucking around, Mr. DJ. Your existence becomes ever more precarious every time my ears are plagued with that opening duh-nuh-nuh-NUH. If I leave you in a pool of your own blood, don't blame me. I warned you. Blame yourself. And "Mississippi Queen."

You talk about yours being a "classic rock" station. In fact, you always refer to your station as "the home of classic rock." The home. Yet with forty fucking years of music to choose from, twice a night you spin some piece-of-shit single that was the number 78 song in the Billboard Top 100 of 1970. I'm looking at the list right now, and it tells me that "Ride Captain Ride" by Blues Image was number 32. I've heard that song about a twentieth as much as "Mississippi Queen." "The Letter" by Joe Cocker is only two spots below "Mississippi Queen," and I have literally heard that song on the radio as many times in my life as I've heard the new Green Day song just today.

Now, I'm not saying that it's a dead certainty that I'm going to slice your penis off and stuff it into your mouth, Mr. DJ. Nothing is inevitable. All you've got to do—and it's real simple—is not play "Mississippi Queen" again. Ever. How hard is that? I mean, with all those decades of music to choose from, all of those great tunes, all that—

Duh-nuh-nuh-NUH! "Mississippi Queen! If ya knoooow what I mean!"

Well, I guess that's it for you then. I'm sorry it had to end this way. But you made your own bed, Mr. DJ. I hope you enjoyed life.

Yo, supervisor? Can I leave a little early tonight?

Classic Rock Songs That Can Go to Hell

Meatloaf, "Two out of Three Ain't Bad"

Foreigner, "Cold as Ice"

The Eagles, "Heartache Tonight"

Jethro Tull, "Aqualung"

The Steve Miller Band, "Abracadabra"

Queen, "We Are the Champions"

Lynyrd Skynyrd, "Sweet Home Alabama"

Billy Joel, "Piano Man"

Journey, "Wheel in the Sky"

Kansas, "Carry On Wayward Son"

Warren Zevon, "Werewolves of London"

Boston, "More Than a Feeling"

Bob Seger, "Old Time Rock and Roll"

Pink Floyd, "Comfortably Numb"

BTO, "Takin' Care of Business"

Golden Earring, "Radar Love"

Aerosmith, "Walk This Way"

Don McLean, "American Pie"

Blue Öyster Cult, "Don't Fear the Reaper"

Elton John, "Crocodile Rock"

Everything by the Doors

I'm Yelling Things from My Car!

"Hey, baby! I know where you want it and I can put it there for you! No? Whatever!"

Yeah, I'm yelling at women from my fifteen-year-old sports car. Yeah, I'm gonna peel out afterward, crank the volume on the stereo, and high-five my friends in the car. And yeah, I'm gonna do it because the noise drowns out the sobbing in my head.

If I was to meet you face-to-face at a club or something, I would avoid eye contact and look into my Long Island iced tea. But look who's avoiding eye contact now!

I have not been with a woman since I was seventeen years old. She was forty-two. I met her after I yelled, "Papa like-y!" and then rode my ten-speed into a ditch because I wasn't watching where I was going. She picked me up out of the ditch, literally, and carried me to her house. There she devoured me as if I were a lamb chop and she were a wolf . . . a wolf the size of a grizzly bear. Hold that thought:

"Okay, you hot slut! I see what you're selling and I want to buy everything you've got in stock! No!? Your loss!"

Instead of a woman, here is a partial list of the things I've made love to: a teddy bear, a sock, a stuffed giraffe, twelve different types of pillows (from goose down to foam), a blow-up doll made to look like a female, a blow-up doll made to look like Antonio Banderas, a raw steak, a banana peel, a chicken breast (cooked because I feared salmonella), a warm Twinkie, and a black velvet unicorn poster.

In high school I had only three friends: Tony, Marco, and Cody. Now I have only two friends, Tony and Cody. Marco ended up being gay, and when he told us I called him a faggot and punched him in the belly. What I really wanted to do was hold him and praise him for the courage to reveal such an emotional elephant to us. But I didn't because of the paralyzing fear in my gut that I find men attractive too. Sometimes I look at Tony's muscular arms and think about how comforting it would be to be held by them. To push out the thought, I drink a bottle of Cutty Sark whiskey and pick fights at the bar. Whoa, here come a couple of good ones:

"What's up, bitches? Want to go for a ride? All the seats in this Chevy Beretta are currently occupied, but I think I could make some room for you . . . on my face! No takers?! Suit yourselves!"

Yeah, I am yelling, "Nice ass!" and "Sweet tits!" at you. Yeah, I will scream, "Stuck-up bitch!" or "Whore!" at you if you ignore me. Yeah, I will shout, "Ohhhhhhh!" if you flip me off or "Spicy mama!" if you tell me to go to hell! No, I don't know what I would do if you actually answered me favorably. I doubt I perform well in bed and would probably cry on the pillow next to you.

Ineffective Lines to Yell at Women from Your Car

I'm overcome by your attractiveness!

Nice jogging shoes!

It's supposed to rain later today!

You resemble my mother from behind!

Engaging in sexual intercourse with you would prove most delightful!

Chase your dreams!

My friends and I are driving in this car!

I'm So Glad You Caught Me, Kid

So this is it, huh? These are my new digs? What was this, a Hellman's jar? Yeah, see, I can tell because it still smells like old, hot mayonnaise in here. So that's nice. I definitely don't see that ever getting old. Man, kid, I'm sure glad you caught me.

Come to think of it, have I even thanked you yet for all that you've done? No? How thoughtless of me. And to think that just a few hours ago I was just bumming around the woods.

After happily wading in a cool, refreshing creek all day, I decided to lazily sun myself on a rock, one of my all-time favorite indulgences that it appears I will never again experience thanks to these handsome new quarters that have so kindly been provided for me.

And thank the Lord you came along to snatch me from my harsh natural surroundings. Speaking of which, you seem a little old to be catching toads. I mean, you're at least thirteen. Shouldn't you be playing football or masturbating or something by now?

Boy, it sure is difficult to believe that this marvelous palace that I now inhabit was until recently wasted on housing a condiment. What a travesty.

So let's take a look at what we've got here, shall we? Okay, looks like I've got about three square inches to move around in. Yeah, I can just barely turn around in here, and it takes a while because my ass is rubbing against the glass. This is going to be a bit of an adjustment, seeing as how until today I had free rein of the entire wilderness and could travel across prairie, glen, and pond whenever my heart desired. But this is good too. It eliminates all that burdensome decision-making about "Where am I going to go today?"

And what else have you done here? Hey look, two leaves! Awesome! You put two leaves in here. I'm assuming those are there to make me feel more comfortable. You're recreating my natural environment. And what a bang-up job too. It's like I never left the woods. Really. And look, you've got a rock in here. Not big enough for me to sit on, but just cumbersome enough to be in my way.

Hey, I know! Why don't you stick a big pinecone in here too? I can still sort of move my right hind leg. Let's remedy that.

I have to admit something to you, little freak boy, and this is rather embarrassing. I was briefly concerned about what I might eat while on display in your sick little budget-ass zoo here. I had some doubts that a twisted little sadist such as yourself would be familiar with the specific dietary requirements of amphibious creatures. But any worries I had were instantly squelched when you crushed up those sour cream and onion Pringles and sprinkled them gingerly into my new home. Soup's on! You fucking spoil me. Do you know that?

And hey, I'd just like to take a moment to apologize for pissing on you when you picked me up. I realize that essentially every creature in the world would recognize that act as a self-defense mechanism that clearly indicates "I don't like what's happening here. Please put me down." However, it seems as though that message went right over your fat, sloped forehead. And thank God it did, or else I might still be out there with my friends, happy, possibly mating.

So what's the game plan? Where do we go from here? Hey, I know! Let's do it this way: You pay attention to me for a couple of days, periodically prodding me with a ballpoint pen and adding new foreign objects to the jar such as spiders and Pepsi, just to see how I'll react. Then, get bored with me and neglect me when you go away for the weekend to visit your aunt in Toledo. I'll just wait here and see if dehydration or starvation claims me first. The race will be on! When you come home and find my tiny dried carcass stuck to the bottom of the jar, just scrape me out and go find some lightning bugs to fuck with for a while. I hear that if you smash them they'll glow on your hands!

I WILL Get Off This Plane Before You

Look, I'm sure you're nice people—we've truly enjoyed your in-flight banter. Your stories about Florida have been interesting, and we really hope your son works out his alcohol problems. But when that "fasten seatbelts" light goes off, you had better stay the fuck out of our way. We WILL get off this plane before you—maybe by as much as thirty or forty-five seconds—or my name isn't Harv Peterson.

It's nothing personal. You just have to understand—we only have one hour to connect to a flight that is nearly seven gates away. And in that time, we must also stop at Starbucks, enjoy a BBQ lunch, check our e-mail, pay our taxes, and pick up the latest copy of *US Weekly*. We can accomplish these things only if we get off this plane as soon as humanly possible—and trust us, we will.

How will we do this? Simple, my friends. When the plane reaches the gate, we will hop up and grab our oversize luggage and make a mad dash down the aisle, pushing and elbowing any passengers or wayward children who get in our way. I will ignore the complaints and insults hurled by the other passengers and I will scream at my wife and berate her mercilessly if I don't think she's moving her ass fast enough.

Honey, prepare to initiate Deboarding Sequence B. Do it NOW! Do you feel that? That's the tension and anticipation building as everyone prepares to collect their belongings and exit the aircraft. Those idiots think this is going to be a civil and orderly process in which they file out row by row, politely allowing others to exit the plane in front of them. Not on my fucking watch. My wife and I are going to storm down that aisle as if it's the running of the bulls!

Yes, I have considered that we are seated near the back of the aircraft. Do you really think that's an obstacle we haven't been confronted with before? One time I was seated thirty-six rows back and still managed to be the first living soul off the plane. I broke some old lady's hipbone, but every war has its casualties. Also, we would have had seats closer to the front if my wife here weren't so incompetent.

Anyway, I hate to cut this short, but I've got a plane full of people to piss off here. The trick is making a huge ruckus from the very beginning so people get the message that we're the kind of assholes who will knock them down if they get in our way.

Honey, get the luggage. Let's go, let's go, MOVE!

Chapter Three
I've Already Got Plans

This Gangbang Is So Awkward

Oh, man. This was not a good idea.

What am I supposed to be doing right now? Should I be doing something? She looks pretty occupied currently. She's already handling three dudes. I guess I'll just stand here and stroke it some more. Keep your head together, Mike. Your time will come. Man, this gangbang is awkward!

This always looked so cool in the videos. But all this waiting and watching is really uncomfortable.

I figured I'd just sort of fall into a natural rhythm and find my groove, but I've gotta admit that I am really perplexed as to the proper gangbang protocol here.

Whoa. She just looked at me. Does that mean she wants me to come up there? Maybe that's what she's indicating. But what if she didn't mean that? What if I go up there and shove my junk in her face and she doesn't want anything to do with it? I'd look like a real horse's ass then. I'd better just wait here.

Man, this guy's taking a long time. Come on, dude, who are you trying to impress here? There are other guys waiting.

Look at that guy's penis! It's way bigger than mine. Thicker at least. I hope I don't have to follow him. She won't even know I'm in there.

Oh, man, he caught me staring at it. That's just great. Now he's gonna think I'm queer. I'm not queer, man. I'm just a little self-conscious. God, this is awkward.

It's too hot in here.

These guys are all saying sexy things to her. I'm the only one who's not talking dirty. I should say something so that they don't think I'm lame. Here goes . . .

"Yeah, you like that, bitch?"

Shit. That was stupid. Now everyone's looking at me like I'm some misogynistic asshole.

I am an asshole. Why did I have to say the most cliché, demeaning thing I could think of? Like I need to remind her that she "likes that." Smooth move, dumbass.

I wonder why she's doing this. I'll bet she had a bad childhood. She probably lacked a strong paternal figure in her life.

Damn it. Now I'm at half-mast. Now I look like the guy that can't keep it up. Concentrate, Mike. Stop psychoanalyzing and keep your mind on the sex.

Okay, here we go, that guy's done. About time. Should I go now? I've waited long enough. I'm going in there.

Damn it. The Italian guy beat me to it. I was here way before the Italian guy. How are we determining whose turn it is here anyway? Was there some sign-up sheet I missed or something? Damn it.

Steady, Mike old boy. There's plenty for everyone. Just wait it out. Deep breaths.

I hope no one tries to go anal when I'm taking my turn. I'm not real cool with my stuff touching another guy's stuff. And I think in that case it would be unavoidable.

Something in here stinks. Is that me? I hope it's not me. Oh, man—I hope it's not her! Wait, no, it's that guy. Thank God.

Time to make your move, Mike. Gotta get in there and mix it up. Otherwise I'm that creep at the gangbang who's just watching and beating off. You've gotta be in it to win it. Here goes.

Wait, what's going on? We're climaxing already? I haven't even gone yet!

Okay, stay calm, Mike. No one knows that. Just finish yourself off so that you're not the odd man out.

Well, this was great. A red-letter day in my sad sexual history. And what am I supposed to do now? Do we all hang around for a while and talk about it? Where should I clean up?

God, this is awkward.

Half of This Relationship Is Not Working

I think we need to talk. I know it's five A.M., but before I go, I just need to get this out. I'm having a real problem with one part of our relationship.

No, the fucking is great. It's the buddy part that I'm not comfortable with.

Remember the night we met? You were at your old sorority sister's bachelorette party. Trish? Tisha? It doesn't matter. Remember how we picked out songs on the jukebox together? You wanted to play Jimmy Buffet. That was my first indication that we might be able to fuck but we'd never become buddies. We're just from two different worlds . . . Hold on, let me take this condom off.

Don't get me wrong, I want to keep fucking you on occasion. I have no complaints in that department. Well, we could do it doggy-style more often, but that's not the point. All I'm saying is, we may be a perfect fit when it comes to fucking, but we just weren't meant to be buddies.

I guess the difference is that I would go to a wedding with a buddy. You see what I mean?

That's right, I'm not going to that wedding with you. Now, if you want to call me after the reception to fuck, that would be perfectly fine. Are you starting to see how this is going to work?

Let me try to explain. The phone calls in the middle of the day—all you do is complain how all the nurses are bitches and the doctors won't give you the time of day. I don't care how stressful it is to be in pharmaceutical sales. I don't want to go out with your bitchy friends, or go see the new Jake Gyllenhaal movie with you. I don't want to get dinner or help you move that dresser. I'm not going to call just to see what's up, so you shouldn't either. That's buddy territory. And the two of us aren't meant to be fuck buddies.

You're just not my type, and I think you even realize that we just wouldn't work as a serious couple. I mean, you refer to me as a friend with benefits, so I know you recognize it. My problem is that I don't really even consider us friends. We've never even seen each other in daylight. That should give you some indication that we're not all that close. We should just stick to what we're good at. Really drunk fucking.

So, to make this relationship work, we're going to have to set some new ground rules.

Just as an example, when you're thinking about calling me, ask yourself these simple questions: Is this call an invitation for fucking? Is this call to solidify plans for fucking? Is this conversation going to lead to fucking in the near future? If the answer is yes, go ahead and call. If the answer is no, I really don't want to hear about it.

Another quick one: After we're done fucking, there doesn't need to be any interaction. I don't want to get you a glass of water. And I'm getting up to leave, not to help you find your underwear. It's not my fault you happen to have an incredible body and a horrible personality. I'm not sure whose fault that is—maybe MTV's or your parents'?

I don't mean to be rude, I'm just being honest. One day you'll find someone who likes Stoli Orange, makeup, and being tan as much as you do. Then the two of you can be the best of buddies as well as fuck. It will happen for you, don't worry. Did you see how many guys tonight had armband tattoos? You see, there's somebody out there that would kill to be your fuck buddy. I just want to fuck.

I hope we understand each other. I hope you know I treasure one aspect of our relationship: the fucking. And I'll always cherish that.

Excuses to Leave After Sex

It's only a fifteen-minute parking meter

Wife's making lasagna tonight

Forgot to TiVo *Two and a Half Men*

VD clinic closes in an hour

Crime ain't gonna fight itself, lady

No, I Don't Feel Any Different

Yes, I got married. Thanks for the congratulations, but please let me stop you before you ask me if it feels any differ—too late. Allow me to respond here so that I don't have to waste another breath answering this idiotic question.

First of all, fuck you.

Second, no, it does not feel any different. Aside from this ring on my finger and a ten-day vacation, everything is exactly the same as it was a few weeks ago. What exactly do you suspect might "feel different"? My wife's vagina? Not that that is any of your goddamn business, but it also feels the same as before.

Emotionally? Is that what you are asking?

I sincerely hope that this is not what you mean. Do I look like a woman? No. Who asks an adult man how he feels? Do you ask a retard what he thinks?

If you are a man asking me the question, sack up and say what you mean: "Do you regret it?" The answer to that question is no. I don't regret it. If I didn't want to get married, I wouldn't have done it. I am not a pussy like you are. And if you ever ask me how I "feel" again, I will punch you in the face.

Now, women, I know why you ask. You like to humiliate men in public by asking them how they feel about things. I get it. We make more money than you and are better at sports, so you talk about emotions, get fat, and cut off your hair.

The truth of it is that men all feel the same thing when their wedding is over: relief. We are just glad that no one had to die, and we hope that there is enough cash in the envelopes to cover the cost of all the bullshit we had to pay for.

The thing that really frustrates me about this question is that its utterance proves that you and I don't really have anything to talk about. Otherwise you wouldn't lead off the conversation with such a stupid fucking question. Where are we going to go from here? I am going to say, "No" while I imagine burning your face off with a flaming log, and then there will be an uncomfortable silence. You will then follow up with an equally inane question, or you will congratulate me again and walk away. Let's skip to part three, and you can just walk away. That way I won't hate you later.

But seriously, thank you for the set of pewter teaspoons. They will go great with the napkin rings and the cheese tray. In the garbage.

Nice to Meet You, Lying Whore

Hey, how's it going? Great party, huh? So where you from?

I guess it really doesn't matter since about eight months from now I'll probably cringe every time the city of your origin is brought up by someone in conversation. But just for shits and giggles, where are you from anyway? Better yet, what do you do for living? This stuff will be good to know because I'm going to hate you and everything about you in about eight months. So let's keep up with this mindless conversation that will eventually lead to us having sex later back at my place. I know you probably don't realize it yet, but you will most likely be the biggest mistake of my life. And with my dating history, that is saying a lot. So can I get you another drink?

How many brothers and sisters do you have? How old is your mom? Where does your dad work again? What was the longest relationship you ever had? Come on, start answering all these questions, because we need to build that spark and force a chemistry that we will be pretending to have in order to justify banging each other in about two hours. Seriously though, I think you're simply "fascinating" because you played "volleyball" in high school, I really do!

Let's take a picture together! Come on, this will be the perfect thing to rip up in eight months when I'm cursing your name at the top of my lungs. CHEESE!

That was fun! We're having so much fun getting to know each other, so are you ready to head back to my place to fuck—I mean, "make love"? Let's hurry, because we only have eight months to go until this is all just a horrible memory that I'll want to erase from my mind forever. Come on, let's roll!

Wow! Sex was great! I can't believe how much we connect as people. I can talk to you all night, so let's do a little pillow talk. Tell me about your family again, because I'm looking forward to coming into their lives, and getting to know them, only to have your father say, "Stay the hell away from my daughter" later on down the road. I hope he's huge. That's going to be awesome!

What else can we do? Oh yeah, do you want to go ahead and cheat on me now, or do you want to wait eight months until I really start developing feelings for you? Better wait. It'll make it more difficult and painful for me that way. But I'm giving you the option to do it now so we can get it out of the way . . . You'll just wait to do it later? That's cool! Well, in that case, let's start falling for each other right now. I can't wait until I have those thoughts about wanting to kill you! Wheee!

So how many kids do you want? It really doesn't matter, because we'll never have them together. Just tell me more about yourself because I want to pretend you're my soul mate some more. Keep on talking about yourself.

Guess what? I have a secret for you. While you were droning on about your ex-boyfriend I was just thinking about how I was going to spend close to four thousand of my hard-earned dollars on you in the months to come. Seriously! I'm going to take you out to fancy dinners at trendy places that I hate. We'll catch a bunch of movies. I'll even periodically surprise you with flowers. Oh, I'm not done, and neither is my Visa check card. I'm going to buy you expensive clothes and spoil you with jewelry, only to look back in eight months on the eight thousand bucks I pissed away into the wind. How perfect is this going to be?

Well, I had better be getting you home. I don't want to keep you out too late. We've got a lot of agony and heartbreak ahead of us to get to, so I want to get a good night's rest. Lord knows I won't have one for a while after this.

So, great! It was so nice meeting you, and I'll call you tomorrow to spend money on you and have sex with you again. And thanks for ruining my life, you soulless wretch!

Bad Girlfriends

"Do you need something off that shelf?"
The tall girlfriend/short boyfriend combo not only makes the couple uncomfortable but kind of creeps out all the people around them. It's just unnatural and it rarely works out—just ask Billy Joel. Maybe it is rooted in man's immature need to feel superior to women, but the mechanics of the lanky sex alone are enough to turn off the majority of men to this type of coupling.

"I have to be honest with you: you're not my first."
This girlfriend usually begins as an attempted one-night stand that manifests into something far more sinister. A few more late-night drunk hookups and the next thing you know, you're in a relationship. And that would be fine if she didn't ever want to leave the house, but it seems that everywhere the two of you go you run into ten different guys who give you the knowing look or blatant admission that they have screwed her ten ways till Tuesday. The majority of your time is now spent eyeing these past gentleman callers up and down in an attempt to determine what heinous diseases they have passed on to you through your germ farm of a girlfriend.

"Can't we just watch Lost_?"_
Having a girlfriend who wants sex everywhere, all the time, is awesome! For a month. After that, it grows a bit wearisome. You've already explored every inch of her body, so there are no more surprises there. You've done it in every conceivable position, including a few that even grossed YOU out a little bit, but still she wants more. Your time is now completely monopolized, because when you're not trying to satisfy her you're at church seeking forgiveness for that thing you did to her with the rubber mallet and the cheese grater the other day.

"I love you sooo much!"

This girl might seem all right at first. She's eager to please in and out of the bedroom, and it's hilarious when she breaks a bottle over the waitress's face for "making eyes at her man." But it won't last long. And when you finally try to break it off, she'll probably kill your dog.

"Let's get high and watch that Phish bootleg."

Hippie chicks have an odd hotness about them—when they are young. There is something attractive about a liberated woman who is, ostensibly, a subscriber to the "free love" philosophy, but without a bra, years of gravity take a toll and that cute peach fuzz on her legs becomes thick, wiry hairs blacker than a thousand midnights. But she can always score the bammer, so . . .

"Love means never having to do anything for myself."

These girls are nothing but arm candy for guys with low self-esteem. We are all real impressed that you scored such a beautiful woman, really, we are. But is the few minutes a week having missionary-position sex with her worth the hours and hours of doing everything from killing a spider to putting gas in her car?

"You have to hear this!"

Not only do these girls not know when to shut the fuck up, every story they tell seems to include a completely unnecessary and excruciatingly long backstory that starts sometime during the Jurassic period and goes on tangentially until you are forced to ask, "What is the goddamn point?" She's almost always hot, and because men have always feigned interest in her stories to try and get into her pants, she has no idea that she is criminally boring.

"I want our first time to be special."

Me too, baby. But I want it to be soon. Adult relationships include sex. Period. Until you have sex, you are just friends. And we all have more than one friend.

My Eighth-Grade Dance: An Open Apology

Dear Mandy,

I know it's been a long time since we've spoken—fourteen years to be exact—but I (as well as my therapist) feel that I probably owe you some long-overdue explanations for a few of the actions that took place on the magical night we spent together.

Before I begin, I would like to once again thank you for taking a chance on a midsemester transfer student during the biggest event of the spring, the 1991 Apollo Junior High Star-Seeker Extravaganza. The sympathy and generosity that you displayed in accepting my three-page handwritten request by checking the "yes" box has not been forgotten, even though Susan Dobson later told me that you accepted only because you had assumed that I was retarded.

Okay, here goes. The things I'm sorry for (chronologically):

6:18 P.M. My mom's "awesome" new car that I promised you we could ride in to the dance. To be fair, I thought the 1988 Ford Festiva had a lot of potential, and if my folks had sprung for air conditioning or even a tape deck, this may not have even made the apology.

6:32 P.M. Getting blood on your new dress. My nose has a tendency to start bleeding when my allergies are acting up or when I get really nervous. It was either the particularly high pollen count or the switchblade your father kept rubbing against his crotch that caused my nostril fountain to unleash its fury on your new ensemble.

7:05 P.M. Not asking you to dance when that Bryan Adams song from Robin Hood was played. It would have been the perfect opportunity, but I thought it was a little too early in the night to blow my load on a slow dance, and also, I was still extremely dizzy from the excessive blood loss.

7:08 P.M. Asking you to dance when "I Wanna Sex You Up" by Color Me Badd was played. I went through five plastic cups of punch during the prior song, building up the nerve to ask you. The song choice was in no way a reflection of my intentions. It was, however, quite the provocative selection by our DJ/gym teacher, Mr. Turmose.

7:41 P.M. Attempting a running man into a handstand during "Gonna Make You Sweat" by C + C Music Factory. Had I known that I would misstep and fall, ramming my head into your ovaries and almost certainly ruining the chance of your ever bearing children, I would have played it a bit safer.

8:09 P.M. Performing what could best be described as a free-form version of the cabbage patch during "Do Me" by Bell Biv DeVoe. Even though you were still being attended to by the school nurse, I could see you sneering at me while I was on the dance floor, alone, flailing my arms about as if I were either boxing a kangaroo or on fire (or boxing a kangaroo who was on fire).

8:22 P.M. Calling you a filthy slut for dancing with Brian Trevorman. I now see that it was premature of me to have assumed that you had been in the bathroom giving him a hand job while I was refilling your punch glass. I had no idea that you tutored him after his special ed. classes, or that he was blind.

8:47 P.M. Trying to feel you up in the backseat of the Festiva on the way home. Admittedly, I underestimated the toll that the night's previous mishaps had taken on our relationship. Also, sorry for calling you a cocktease (though I stand by that assertion).

Thank you for taking the time to read this. Before I go, a couple other things I forgot to apologize for:

Telling you I was as "Cool as Ice." Turns out I wasn't.

Telling you that my MC Hammer pants were imported from Italy. They were actually just Zubaz that my grandma had bought from the sale rack at Marshall's.

Shaving your name into my head beneath a Nike swoosh logo. I really can't explain this one.

Again, very sorry,
Brandon Gnetz

P.S. Also, really sorry about driving by your house four to five times a night wearing a cheerleading outfit that I accidentally took from your gym locker. That was in high school, though, and may require its own letter.

Junior High Dating Tips

Playing in the woods is more of a third-date activity. On your first date, ride bikes.

When engaging in braces-on-braces kissing, concentration is the key to avoiding entanglement.

When thieving from Dad's liquor cabinet to help "set the mood," remember that dry vermouth and triple sec make better mixers than stand-alone drinks.

Asking her when she thinks her boobs might come in is never appropriate conversation.

Date fifth-graders. Less baggage.

Welcome to Every Date Ever

Knock knock.

Oh, hi, how's it going? It's me! Every girl ever. I'm really looking forward to this date. I'm not nearly as attractive as you remember me being because when we met the bar was dark and you were drunk. Come on in.

Let's start off with the unavoidable tour of my incredibly typical post–college girl apartment.

You'll notice that I went ahead and purchased everything that Ikea and Pier 1 have ever produced. There's my decorative birdcage over there even though I don't have a bird, and there's my gay wicker basket with bamboo poles in it. I don't know what the hell that thing's all about, but I bought it.

Hey, check it out—I have more candles in here than a Roman Catholic church. Doesn't it smell like hazelnut!? If I were to light all my candles at once you could see my apartment from space. I fucking love candles!

Come on into the living room.

Oh, I see you met my cat there. That's Freddy Paws Jr. Why don't you pet him and act like you like cats even though you hate cats? There you go. Oh, he took a little swing at your eye there, huh? Yeah, he'll do that. Hey, let's check out the kitchen.

Look at my refrigerator. There are pictures all over it. Look at all these pictures of me and my equally vacuous friends from college. We were so crazy! You can tell we're really good friends because our faces are all pressed up against each other like that.

And see? We're holding alcoholic beverages up to the camera in every single picture. That's to prove that we were partying. College was so fun! But of course I don't talk to any of these girls anymore because now they're all bitches.

Hey, before we leave, I'm going to go into the bathroom for ten minutes for some mysterious reason. Why don't you sit awkwardly in my big, stupid round papason chair over there while you wait for me. It's like you're sitting in a hug! Be right back . . .

Sorry that took a half an hour—I don't know what the hell I was doing in there. Let's go!

Wow! Thanks for opening my car door for me! I'm totally going to blow that meaningless gesture out of proportion and delude myself into thinking that you're a really good guy, because that's what I want to believe.

Well, here we are at the restaurant. No thanks, waiter, I don't need to see a menu, just bring me some expensive things. Hey, I know, while we wait, I'll tell you all about my unspeakably boring job. I hate my boss. He's a jerk! I might get another job. Maybe something in pharmaceutical sales.

Now let's talk about my family. I love my family. I want you to love my family. I want my family to love you. I want you to make love to my family! I want you to go golfing with my semi-retarded brother, Travis. That would be so god-damned cute!

Wow! I can't believe I ordered all this food! I have no intention of eating any of it. No thanks, waiter, we don't need a box. Just throw it out.

Hey, I've got an idea! Let's go to a bar and have an after-dinner drink! It'll be great—it will be just like how we're drinking here, only it will be louder and we'll have to stand up. Come on!

See, isn't this better? Oh, hey, what a coincidence. Look over there! It's a group of my friends that I knew was going to be here. Let's go over there so they can judge you!

Hey, I have to go to the bathroom for a half an hour again for some reason. You can stay here and talk to my unbelievably hideous friend Christine! Christine's so ugly, she scares kids! Talk to her! She has a job and a family that she wants to talk to you about too. Be right back.

I'm back! Sorry I was gone for three hours, there was a line. I want to go home now.

Well, here we are at my door again. This was really fun for me and not you. You should pretend like we're going to do it again sometime! Maybe I'll see you at Target a few months from now and we can avoid eye contact because you never called me. Here, have this awkward goodnight kiss that's as empty as my soul. Good night!

Darling, If You Really Loved Me, You'd Bleach Your Asshole

Hey, honey? Remember how we had that talk the other night while we were falling asleep about how great it was that we could talk to each other about anything? And remember how you said that you love doing stuff that makes me happy? Do you also remember how my birthday is right around the corner?

Okay, I'm just stalling now. I'm just going to say it. Here goes.

It would mean a whole lot to me if you would have your anus professionally whitened.

I knew you were going to react like that. It's like when I comment on your driving—you get all sensitive and bent out of shape.

Settle down. No, there's nothing wrong with your asshole. I love your asshole. I think I've proven that over time. But after years of wear and tear and, well, just being an asshole, it could use a little downtown cosmetic assistance.

The procedure is a breeze, babe! I've been reading about it online a lot at work lately, which, incidentally has led to some pretty sweeping changes in office policy regarding on-the-clock Internet use.

First they do a little laser treatment hair removal, "groundskeeping," so to speak, which, let's face it, would not be a complete waste of time for you, my little Italian princess. Then, once the table is set, they simply apply the bleach throughout the course of three or four sessions, depending on the current darkness of your anus and your desired level of whiteness.

I say we go with the four.

No, I'm not making it up. Everyone is doing it right now. It's the hot new thing. What do you mean, "who"? You want names? Fine: Devon, Jenna, Asia Carrera. What? Yes, they're all porn stars. So what? Are you saying that they don't count as people just because you don't agree with their choice of profession? That's pretty elitist. How about you come down off that high horse for a minute?

And say what you will about those girls, but at least their anuses don't look like a wink from a guy who lost a bar fight.

Now let's talk cost. As it is a fairly expensive procedure, I was hoping that you would check to see if your health-care plan at work would cover it. You're pretty sure it doesn't? Have you even looked? I didn't think so. Would you at least ask around at work?

Look, I don't remember putting up a big argument a couple of months ago when you made me get rid of my goatee. And I loved that thing. It hid my weak chin. But it was important to you, so I shaved off a big part of who I was in order to make you happy. That's starting to look like a big mistake right about now, isn't it? I guess I just wasn't aware that this relationship was a one-way street.

And that was something that everyone could see. Your physical improvement could be our little secret. It could be just between me and you and a select few of my friends who I would want to have check it out.

Fine, no friends! Jesus. You used to be fun.

Can't You Just Get a Cab to the Abortion Clinic?

Look, I'm not trying to be a prick here, and I know that this is probably a pretty tough time for you and all, but if there is some way around me driving you to the abortion clinic, that would be really cool, 'cause I'm, like, super busy.

Okay, I'm not so much "busy" as I am "hung over." But regardless, I am not in what you would call a "driving mood" right now.

And really, I don't see any difference between my taking you and your grabbing a cab. In fact, you'll probably get there faster. You know how I am with directions, and cab drivers know how to get anywhere. You already MapQuested it? Now, you know those directions are never reliable, babe. I think I'd just feel safer if you were with a sober, clearheaded driver with a working knowledge of the streets rather than me. I'm really thinking of you here.

You know, now that I think about it, I don't see any reason why you can't just drive yourself to the clinic. From what I recall, the procedure is amazingly quick and relatively painless. These aren't the Dark Ages anymore. Abortion science has taken huge leaps in recent years. You're in, you're out. It's like the dentist. My last girlfriend and I went bowling that same night. Well, I bowled. She just watched and kept my score.

I don't know why you don't want to drive. That's the funny thing about women. You gals are always squawking about how you want equal rights and saying how you don't need us for anything, and then as soon as you hit a little bump in the road you're all, "I really need you to be here for me right now." Women's lib, my ass.

Look, not to get nitpicky, but I'm already paying for half the procedure. That's a hundred and fifty bucks. And now I have to be your personal chauffeur too? I'd say I've paid my dues. You don't think I could use that money for something else? A hundred and fifty bones might not mean much to you Miss Target Manager, but that could have been two badly needed new tires for the old Chevy Cavalier. But I guess you're cool with me driving around on bad wheels. Winter's right around the corner, you know.

Okay, I'm going to say this one more time, and I already know your stance on it, but just hear me out. I say we wait on this for just a little while longer. It's a statistical fact that the majority of miscarriages happen within the first two months. I say we roll the dice and wait it out a bit. Because really, when you think about it, what is a miscarriage but a free abortion?

Not to be insensitive, but this whole situation really burns me up. It's like I'm paying a hundred and fifty bucks for sex. I could have gotten a prostitute for that kind of money. The only difference is that a hooker would have the common sense to remember to take her pill.

Oh, great. Here come the waterworks. Look, I didn't mean to make you cry. I was just trying to make a point. Geez. Your chick hormones must be working overtime right now. You're super touchy.

Women's Legitimate Reasons to Have an Abortion

Plane tickets for Panama City spring break nonrefundable

Lots of stress at work right now, not a good time to quit smoking

Conflicts with summer weight-loss plan

Not totally convinced that the child is even mine

Just saw *The Omen* and don't want to take outside chance of birthing the Antichrist

Want to show support for *Roe v. Wade*

Send a message to my other kids that I am not to be fucked with

Why Must You Always Be So Negative?

Honey, I really think we need to have a serious talk about your attitude. I just don't understand why you insist on being so negative all the time. I mean, take this "petition for divorce" that you just sent me. It's oozing with negativity from page 1. Hell, look at the way it starts:

1. By and through this petition, Petitioner BRENDA ECKHARDT, an adult citizen of Essex County, seeks a divorce and a permanent order of protection against Respondent DENNIS J. ECKHARDT, on the grounds of adultery, physical abuse, bigamy, public humiliation, animal cruelty, and attempted murder.

You see, right from the get-go you focus on all the bad stuff. It's like you want everyone who reads this to think I'm some kind of scary guy. But we both know there's a lot more to me than banging babysitters and clocking you in the face.

I mean, come on now, honey—bigamy? We've been over that one like a gazillion times. You know I never considered Lisa to be a regular wife. I only married her because she was pregnant, and I remembered how bad you felt for your friend Tina when her husband had a kid with that woman from his job. You kept saying that you couldn't imagine "the shame" of having a husband who had an illegitimate child—I married Lisa only to spare you that shame. But now you and this lawyer of yours are trying to turn it around into something negative. I'd be lying if I said I wasn't a little hurt by that.

And then there's the part in paragraphs 32 and 33 about your supposed "public humiliation":

32. On or about July 17, 2003, after a night of binge drinking, respondent DENNIS J. ECKHARDT returned home with several intoxicated friends. With the help of at least two of these friends, Respondent attempted to create a videotape showing Respondent flatulating in Petitioner's face while she slept.

33. However, Respondent apparently misjudged the fullness of his lower intestine and sprayed several pieces of fecal matter onto the face and neck of Petitioner. Respondent later uploaded a video clip of this incident onto an Internet Web site entitled www.shitsandgiggles.com. As of the date of this Petition, said video clip was still available for viewing by the public.

Now, you know that's not the whole story. You didn't mention the two hundred bucks the Web site paid us for the video, and how at least three of those dollars were spent on those tampons you supposedly "needed."

And then there's this part at the end about how "on or about September 19, 2004, Respondent became severely intoxicated after losing a football bet. In his drunken stupor, Respondent mistook Petitioner for placekicker Sebastian Janikowski of the Oakland Raiders, who earlier in the day had missed a 37-yard field goal attempt that resulted in the Raiders' failure to cover the spread . . ."

64. Enraged by the loss of his $300 wager, Respondent forced Petitioner to remove all her clothes and then proceeded to spray-paint Janikowski's jersey number (11) onto Petitioner's naked torso. Respondent then forced Petitioner—at gunpoint—to stand in front of the couple's garage door during a hailstorm while Respondent placed logs of firewood on a tee and kicked them at Petitioner as he shouted, "Take that, you fat Polack!"

65. Angered by his inability to hit Petitioner with any of the logs, Respondent then discharged his firearm several times in Petitioner's direction. After emptying the ammunition cartridge of his gun, Respondent hurled the weapon toward Petitioner and collapsed on the ground.

All right, I suppose you got me on that one. But the rest of this thing is just so unfair. For the sake of your own happiness, I really think you need to start looking at the bright side of life and stop playing the blame game.

Maybe when you stop being Polly Pessimist you'll realize that everything that went wrong in our marriage was your fault.

I Want You to Be in My Wedding!

Great news! I got engaged! I know, crazy, right? I want you to come to my wedding, buddy. It's in, like, a year. It's going to be great. I want you and your lovely girlfriend to come. The bar will be open, my friend. You want the chicken or the steak?

Since we're pretty tight, I want you to be in the wedding. I want you to be a part of what will be an awesome day, my friend.

Me and the fiancée (its *sooo* weird saying that word!) have lots of planning to do and we've set dates for just about everything, so there are a few things we need to discuss.

The engagement party will be next month. It's going to be awesome! It's only a two-and-a-half-hour drive for you, and it's gonna be a sick time. You might want to grab a hotel room for that night. Please, no gifts. We're registered at Macy's, Crate & Barrel, and Sears.

There will be three showers in the months ahead. Her family's, my family's, and her friends'. You're obviously excused from those, buddy, but it would be awesome if your girlfriend could make an appearance at all of them. Except, we will want you to come to the Jack and Jill party. We don't expect any gifts from you guys, but again, we are registered, and if you guys want to kick in for one or two of the showers that'd be great!

I hope your girlfriend can make it to the bachelorette party. The gals are heading down to New Orleans for Mardi Gras!

As for the bachelor party, I was hoping you could put that together. I am definitely thinking Vegas. Maybe the Palms, I don't know. I hear the Real World suite is pretty awesome! Surprise me!

I already found a great deal on some awesome tuxedos. They are only $250 each, just as long as we have them back by six A.M. the day after the wedding.

The rehearsal dinner will be the night before the wedding. The rehearsal will be a few hours . . . my fiancée is Greek Orthodox, so there is a lot of crazy Greek stuff to go over. They do everything three times. It so weird, and takes so long. Very interesting stuff!

The church is so cool. It's really rustic. It was built like two hundred years ago. It's so amazing! It's definitely not air-conditioned, so wear something light. Wait, strike that—you'll be in a black wool tuxedo! What was I thinking?

The ceremony will only be about two hours, unless she decides she wants to do the lighting of the unity candle ritual, which would push it to about two and a half. That's still up in the air.

Then the party will commence! After the pictures, of course. We have the best wedding photographer. She is kind of a perfectionist, very meticulous. But the best things come to those who wait! Right?

The reception is going to be sick! By the time we are done taking pictures, we should have a good solid hour or two to get introduced, have our dances, do the speeches and toasts, eat some apps, salad, soup, main course, a little drinky or seven, and then the cake. It's going to be the best wedding ever!

My brother, who's the best man, has a huge fear of speaking in public. Can you do the best man speech? Thanks, man. I appreciate it. Don't go out of your way, though. Ten, twelve minutes tops, okay? And I'll just need to proofread it first. And I'll help you with your timing.

You're probably going to need a hotel room for the weekend, on account of the brunch the morning after. I would return your tux first, then be back for the eight A.M. brunch. You will absolutely love the rooms there—they are super luxurious!

Of course, you won't need a hotel room if you have family down there. I doubt you have family in Antigua, though. Let me tell you, my friend, you are going to see plenty of that island! The tux place, the church, and the hotel are spread out all over the place! Airplane tickets are actually pretty cheap right now, and I've seen a few with only two or three layovers. It will be hurricane season down there, so pack some extra clothes, just in case we all get stuck for a week or so!

I need to ask you what you want as a gift from the groom (me!). I was thinking maybe a pen. Do you have a good pen? Not a great pen but decent one, anyway. Do you have a pen that works?

Send your RSVP back as soon as possible, because if you guys can't make it, I need to get someone from the B list. We need asses in the seats! I'm so happy for us!

Chapter Four

I Gotta Catch the Game, Bro

Dear Chris Berman

Dear Chris Berman,

I just wanted to drop you a line to let you know that I am your biggest fan. Whereas other people might say that your acts are tired and unfunny, I am here to tell you—keep doing your thing. Those acts that people say are worn out have been working for the last fifteen years, so why stop now?

Some people even have the nerve to say that ESPN has gone downhill. I say hogwash. As long as you're still with the network, it will be the only place I go to get my sports coverage. Sometimes I think that ESPN stands for "Every Sports Program Needs . . . some Chris Berman." Wouldn't life be grand if we could hear your shtick all the time?

Personally, I think the nicknames that you do are downright hysterical. Chuck "New Kids on" Knoblauch is top-shelf comedy any way you slice it. Think about how much that sounds like "New Kids on the Block." I'd like to see your critics come up with such a perfect combination of humor, sports, and NKOTB.

I always laugh when I hear you say Julius "Salt and" Peppers or Albert "Winnie the" Pujols. Some people may think you're just stubbornly refusing to accept that you aren't funny anymore by continuing to use the same jokes you used in 1987, but I'm not one of those people.

Sportscenter *would be so much better if you were back on there doing it every day. And the same goes for ESPNews. Who wants to just see highlights with no jokes mixed in? Bo-ring!*

My favorite show on the network has to be NFL Primetime. *No surprise why that is! Most of the time people who cover the NFL just show highlights and expect the game itself to provide the excitement. Who wants to see just football highlights and scores? I want to be entertained.*

All sportscasters should watch you do highlights so they can get a clue how to make them fun. I just can't wait until you do the "rumblin', bumblin', stumblin'," thing and, sure enough, every show you do it. I also love that you still say "Marshall, Marshall, Marshall!" when Marshall Faulk is running the ball. I used to not know his first name, but after eight years of that joke, now I sure do!

That Swami character you've created is just brilliant. Who cares if you are wrong on 90 percent of the games? Those little sketches are so funny that one time I actually urinated on myself while watching.

If that wasn't enough, I consider it a second Christmas every year when you do the All-Star Game Home Run Derby. My year isn't complete until I hear you go, "Back, back, back, back" at least fifteen times per batter. You say it so fast!! As far as I'm concerned, when it comes to comedy, it's Gallagher, Louie Anderson, and Chris Berman—then everyone else.

Don't listen to the haters. The people who think that you aren't the best thing ever to happen to ESPN just don't understand true genius when they see it. I just want to tell you to keep up the stellar work. Now get back, back, back to work!

Sincerely,
Chris Berman

P.S. Check out this cool drawing I did of you . . .

Cheer for Them and I Will Punch You

Hey, douchebag! Yeah, you, down in row 28! The fuck do you think you're doing out here?! This is a Rockies game, and you think you're just gonna show up wearing that faggy blue Royals shit? You better watch your ass, 'cause if you cheer for the opposing team, I will punch you in the face!

You must think I don't take this shit seriously. You see my backwards visor and fake platinum chain? That's serious, champ, and I ain't above handing out an ass-whooping to some nancy-boy who makes the mistake of showing up in Denver and disrespecting my Rockies! Whoa, buddy! Those sunglasses don't scare me! Yeah, that's what I thought—you don't want any of this!

Yo, I don't care if you're just trying to "enjoy the game with your son"; you're wearing the opposing team's colors, and that's a sign of war! You think I'm kidding with you? Then maybe you could tell me why me and my buddies have been pounding Wild Turkey shots in the parking lot since nine this morning—so we can be prepared to deal with jokers like you!

Would you look at that—your little wussy son is crying. Waah waah, Daddy, why does the big scary man hate us? Because you're wearing the colors and logo of the opposing team, you snot-faced little brat! This is the major leagues and my team is the BEST!

Tell you what, Sally. Take off your shirt and I won't give you the beating of a lifetime here in front of your son. How old is he? Six? Yeah, he doesn't need to see firsthand the kind of brain damage I'm about to hand you for wearing that stupid fucking Royals jersey to my precious Coors Field. Speaking of Coors—hey, Lonnie! Throw me another bullet so I can wash down these garlic fries before beating the shit out of this loser!

Oh, so that's how you're gonna do this? You're gonna call security? Fine! It ain't the first time, and it ain't gonna be the last! Lonnie, double time on the Coors. I gotta chug one down before the fuzz gets here. Hurry, here they come now!

Hey, Mike. Steve. Do me a favor and try to keep the cuffs loose this time, if you would. Thanks.

GO ROCKIES!!!

My Fantasy Football Team Is Unstoppable

Fantasy football! Oh yeah, baby! Fantastic. For the record, I am in first place in my money league. Did you hear that? First place. Impressed? You should be. Sure, my team is pretty good—Edgerrin James, Kerry Collins, Tampa Bay defense. But aside from that, who do you think is the one making the shrewd moves? Who is looking his opponent square in the eye and saying, "I'm starting Deion Branch?" That's right . . . this guy!

You know, what's crazy is that I'm only spending about twenty to thirty hours a week on my fantasy league team. Wait until I'm doing it full-time. I'd like to hear people then. I bet people won't be yelling "Nice Life!" or "You're a douchebag." You know what I'd say to them? Scoreboard.

Word around the NFL horn is that I am in the running to replace Mike McCarthy when he is fired in Green Bay. That's right. Take a look at me now, Ms. "You Smell Like Failure." I'm glad we broke up. Best thing that ever happened to me and my team. Pretty soon I'll be smelling like something else. A winner. You see that officially licensed NFL merchandise? I'll have a whole closetful. And the closet will be on my yacht.

Does my success surprise me? No. You know why? One word: guts. I got it and the NFL needs it. I'll tell you what I'll do when I get there too. I'll trade Favre and Driver for Pittsburgh's defense. Straight up! Oh, you heard me correctly. The boys on *NFL Countdown* won't know what hit them. Ditka will be yelling and spitting trying to make sense of my trade. Boomer's head will explode. You think I care? If they were in my fantasy league, they'd know who they were messing with. I'm 3 and 0. A perfect season isn't just possible, it's almost assured.

See, the difference between me and the average fantasy league coach is that those guys see Randy McMichael going into a bye week and worry that their only tight end is not playing. Not me. I stayed in this weekend, got myself a meatball sub, and went to work, and you know what I came up with? Ernie Conwell, baby! Read that again. Ernie Conwell. So you've heard of Ernie Conwell, eh? Did you call him at home? Well, I did. I asked him how he felt. How things were going at home. What his favorite food was, everything. Let me tell you, he sounded pretty angry and threatened to kick my ass. Some people would be scared of that. But you know what? I didn't hear fear . . . I heard fire. Ernie's ready for Sunday and so am I.

You know why I'm so good? No distractions. Do I have a wife? No. Kids? Nope. Girlfriend? Negative. Dates of any kind? Not a one. I stay focused. Those things are just distractions. Take last Thursday, for example. When I was leaving the office, Jim, who's in one of my leagues, was going out for drinks with a couple of these younger girls in the office. He walks by me, winks, and says, "Looks like it's going to be a late night." When does he have time to check the scouting reports? How does he find out that Chicago is two and nine, playing at home after playing an away game in the rain the week before? He doesn't. That's why he's a loser. That's why they are all losers. Make fun of me all you want. You'll be doing it from second place.

I Am So Naked in This Locker Room

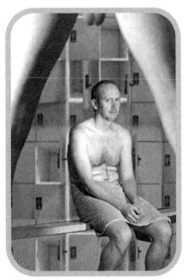

It's about that time, I suppose. Better get to it. Time to walk around this locker room completely naked. After all, I've got a reputation to keep up.

No time like the present to be totally nude in front of a bunch of grown men. Figure I'll walk around awhile, maybe shower, maybe not. I'm going to play that by ear.

No thanks. Don't need a towel. Towels are necessary only after either showering or working out. In both cases they are used to sop up liquid from one's body. As I have yet to exercise or shower, I have no need for a towel at this time. I'm just a naked dude standing in the locker room.

I really want to get a dialogue going with some of these guys. Not people I know, mind you—I have no friends here. I just want to shoot the bull with some random people while standing in front of them. See what's shakin' on their end.

Anybody see that Lakers game last night? How much higher are these gas prices going to get? It's supposed to cool off this weekend, and that is okay by me.

Hey. Guys. Look at me when I'm talking to you. I'm standing right here, just a foot away, with my hands on my hips. How about a little acknowledgment here? Think I'll put my foot up on this bench.

Aaah. There it is. That's better. No avoiding my package now, fellas. It is officially on display. It's like you're all at the Cock Zoo and I've got the least popular exhibit.

Truth be told, as you may have guessed, I'm fifty years old and I have no business whatsoever walking around naked at all, anywhere, at any time. Hell, even my wife tells me to keep my shirt on when we're having sex. If this were a just and fair country, legislation would be passed to ensure that I remain fully clothed at all times—even when showering alone at my house—for the good of the nation.

But this is America, darn it! So it's my right as a citizen and a YMCA three-month-free trial-membership cardholder to walk around naked as the day I was born, a traumatic day in itself, so I have been told.

I Am So Naked in This Locker Room

Hell, I might not even work out today. I might just stay in the locker room the whole time, walking around completely naked. Everyone at some point will have to glance at my unit. The temptation will be there. They'll feel it. Their eyes will crawl down my "happy trail," and, try as they might, they won't be able to stop there.

Only one person is going to be deprived of a good look at my sad little unit, and that would be me. Unfortunately, my gut is completely in the way. I haven't seen my Don Johnson since I was about twenty. Therefore, all my personal knowledge regarding my penis is based on my memory, hearsay, and public response. But I know it's down there. I just gave it a good squeeze.

Hey, as long as I'm here, I think I'll shave naked by the sink. People will definitely have to look at me then. There's no way around it; the sink is right by the locker room entrance. The first thing they will see when they walk into the locker room is the puckered flesh of my bare ass. They won't be able to miss me. And it's pretty narrow right there. They're liable to bump their pelvis into my ass when they try to casually squeeze through. That should be plenty uncomfortable. They might even turn around and walk out, hoping I'll leave soon.

Yeah, right! I'm not going anywhere. I will walk around this locker room naked all day long. They will physically have to put clothes on me and throw me out the door if they want me to leave. And no one has the *cojones* to do that.

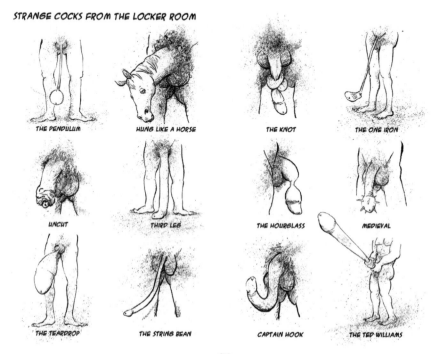

STRANGE COCKS FROM THE LOCKER ROOM

THE PENDULUM   HUNG LIKE A HORSE   THE KNOT   THE ONE IRON

UNCUT   THIRD LEG   THE HOURGLASS   MEDIEVAL

THE TEARDROP   THE STRING BEAN   CAPTAIN HOOK   THE TED WILLIAMS

I'm a Real Fan

My team needs me. That's why I always wear my uniform to every game. I was once like you. Jeans or khakis. A striped shirt. Some loafers. Been there, done that. Two games I attended draped in nondescript street clothes. You know what our record was in the games where I was selfish and dressed like a civilian clown? We were 0–2. Two losses placed squarely on my shoulders. All my fault. From that day on I vowed to never get dressed in the morning without putting on a uniform. Whether I'm going to a game or not.

Regardless, I'm still supporting the team. Because I'm the real deal. Look at you with your suit and your tie. Your allegiance is to no one. Meanwhile, here I am, walking the street wearing my authentic Reebok jersey just like the players wear so that everyone knows where I stand. I'm not afraid to support my team.

I wear my uniform every day, everywhere. If it's coffee at Starbucks, I'm in my uniform. Pumping gas at the filling station, I'm in my uniform. Midday nap on the davenport, I'm in my uniform. Yet society seems to be unwilling to accept this. I'm sorry that my metal cleats are fucking up your floor, and I'm real sorry that they make that annoying clicking sound, but understand this: we've got a championship to win, and I want to do my part.

Let's start with the head. Depending on the season, there can be any number of things paired with my balding coif. Anyone can wear a ball cap promoting their favorite team, but I usually try to take it a step farther. During baseball season I usually don a batting helmet and catcher's mask. During football season, I go with an authentic NFL helmet or an oversize foam helmet at a minimum. During basketball season I go headband. A lot of people make the mistake of painting their faces, but since the pros don't do it, neither do I. Eye black and tattoos are the only acceptable thing that should ever appear on a fan's face.

All my jerseys are custom-made: number 35 (the number of chicks I've banged) with my last name on the back . . . G-R-E-E-N-L-E-A-F. A lot of people make the mistake of wearing their favorite player's jersey, but you are not him, so let's not be ridiculous and get carried away pretending to be a sports hero.

Those players go out there and give their all every time out. You gotta do the same for them. I know I do. Otherwise, why would I be wearing my jersey right now at work? This is not even remotely close to being within the limits of the

I'm a Real Fan

National City Bank dress code. I've been warned twice. I'd say there's a pretty good chance I'll get the ax this time. But does that stop me? You tell me. Am I wearing baseball pants and turf shoes? Check. Stirrups? You bet. Wanna do a cup check? Go ahead, kick me in the balls if you don't trust me. I'm protected. Because I'm a real fan.

High School Football Is All I Have

It's that time of year again. High school football is back in full swing. And I like the look of our North Royalton Purple Raiders this year.

We are coming off a deplorable five-and-five season, and I put the blame squarely on last year's "coach," John Gillen. To this day I have no idea how he even managed to get five wins, what with his head being shoved entirely up his ass. Gillen had this ridiculous "everyone gets to play" strategy that crippled us throughout the season. It's a nice sentiment and all, but let's be realistic. Some of these kids are just weak, valueless sideline gawkers. And they should be brushed aside to make way for the stronger, better people in the same manner that they will be throughout their lives. Gillen just didn't understand that.

Some people were upset when I organized the effort to have the seventy-year-old man removed from his coaching position, but we'll see if I'm still a "meddlesome asshole" when we take Division III State this year.

I like this new coach. Coach Rhodes. He brought back the three-a-day summer practices that Coach Gillen got rid of. And that's what you've gotta do to compete. After all, why should these teenage boys spend their summers with their family and friends, creating memories and experiencing fulfilling and healthy youths, when they can be out in the sun all day running ladders and pushing sleds?

As you might have guessed, I played a little Raider ball back in my day. Defensive back. Led the team in tackles six games my senior year. Probably would have played college ball too if I hadn't knocked up Sue when I was eighteen. My promising football career was cut short by the birth of my faggot son Bill Swayze, Jr.

I have long since given up on trying to get Bill Jr. to play football. I sometimes believe that he has made it his mission in life to disappoint me in every possible manner. Bill Jr. plays soccer. My primary regret in life was granting him the use of my now tarnished name. Early on in his high school career, after much verbal and physical encouragement, Bill Jr. offered to try to make the football team as a punter. I told him that I'd rather he not play at all.

But I don't want to think about that right now. I'd rather concentrate on this year's State-bound Raiders.

Take our quarterback, Chris Pirigyi, for example. Now there is a thoroughbred. Six-one, 185 pounds. The kid is made out of granite. And what a cannon. Now there's a son a father could be proud of. I actually checked his birth records to see if there was any chance that he was born the same day as Bill Jr. I thought there was an outside chance there might have been a mix-up at the hospital. But Chris was born in October, so that theory's out. I really thought we had the same eyes.

I'm a little worried about our cornerback situation this year. We've got this sophomore, Dave Heltzel, who's got a lot of heart, but at five-four and 123 lbs., he's got me a little concerned about his size. I made the offhand remark to Coach Rhodes that while steroid use might be a hot-button issue at the professional level right now, as far as I know they are not currently testing high school players. He got all steamed and told me that was an "outrageous" idea. But I still say that sometimes you have to get your hands a little dirty if you want to build a shrine to greatness.

Recently I've been scouting the practices of every high school team in the area. It's pretty obvious that Garrettsville is going to be a pushover again this year, but I'm not liking what I'm seeing over at the Broadview Heights playing field. It got awfully "dark" over there since last year, if you get my drift. And you know what that means—speed.

This could be a legitimate problem, since the best kid in our secondary, Corey Hoover, got grounded by his father when he caught him drinking and driving this summer. Says he can't play ball this year. So I went over to the Hoover house to try to talk some sense into Tom Hoover, whom I do not know.

I told him that when we were kids we all had our fair share of monkeyshines, and that while punishing Corey is one thing, by not letting him play football he was actually punishing the Purple Raiders fan base as a whole.

Tom, who apparently lacks both parenting skills and school spirit, told me to get the hell off his porch before he called the authorities.

God, that Chris Pirigyi is a stud. He could probably throw the ball two hundred yards if he were so inclined. I wish to Christ he'd knock up my daughter. Imagine that offspring. The kid would get my genetic football smarts and Chris Pirigyi's Adonis-like body. The Colts would probably sign him out of preschool.

But no. My daughter has to date a band geek. Plays drums or some shit. Just my luck. That little fucker eats on the porch when he comes over here for dinner, I'll tell ya that much.

Some people might consider it sad that my overall happiness revolves around the physical accomplishments of a group of teenage boys. Most of these kids can't even vote, but they are directly responsible for my mental well-being and whether or not my wife and queer son get physically abused each Friday night throughout the autumn. But we all have to hang our hat on something.

Think I'll head over to the Brunswick High field to see how they're shaping up this year. Heard they've got a nose tackle the size of a house. That I've gotta see.

I Love the Gym

I can't wait to work out today. I'm going to do chest and biceps. Actually, I think I'll do tris and lats, or maybe legs and abs. Fuck it, I'm lifting everything! I'll do sixteen sets of everything today. It doesn't matter. I love weights. I wish I could lift them all!

God, I love the gym. I'm probably going to stay here all day because I love working out so much.

I'm going to make incredibly obnoxious noises so the entire gym knows I'm lifting heavy weights. I can bench press 350 pounds. I can squat 500 pounds! Everyone will know this before I leave the gym today.

Jesus, my tan looks great under these lights! I think I'll step it up to four times a week and a couple extra minutes in the bed. I tan naked. The tan makes my johnson look bigger.

Is that pansy looking at me? I can't blame him. I look incredible. I'll flip this god-damn forty-five-pound weight around like a coin so he knows how much stronger I am than he is. That's right, pussy . . . look away.

Is that a mirror? I'll look in it from the corner of my eye so no one knows I'm looking at myself. God, I wish I could look at myself dead-on right now. Look at my biceps! They look so huge today. I know other people are checking them out, and I'll just let them. I don't blame them one bit. My arms are enormous.

Oh, damn, check out that chick. She wants me. She wants to touch these arms. I'd let her touch them if she asked. That's right, honey, get a good look. Soak it in. Check out these huge delts, babe. No, up here! Shit, I think she just checked out my package. Dammit! I wish there was a machine for working out your pe-nis. If there was, my cock would be the size of a Volkswagen! It doesn't really matter . . .

I'm so cut everywhere else. My chest and my arms are ripped!

I need more supplements right now. After I finish here I'm going straight to GNC. Those guys have my order memorized. I just drop my GNC gold card on the counter and they throw my stuff in a bag.

One more set and then it's time for a protein shake. It helps my muscle re-covery.

I'm Going to Run onto the Field

Man, this game is boring. I'm fucking hammered and I still can't enjoy this. There is nothing worse than a 6–1 game in the sixth inning. Nothing. We did the wave already and that sucked. They already showed the bloopers between innings. There's nothing left to do. Shit, I should just run onto the field.

Wait, that's it! I should do that. Why not? I have always gotten a kick out of seeing it happen in the past. It's the ultimate game of cat and mouse. An undermatched, inebriated fan against fired-up security guards who have just been waiting for someone to test them. Today I will be that someone!

So that's it—I'm going to do it. I have no idea what I'll do when I get out there, but I'll improvise. Maybe I'll slide into second, or third, even. Yeah, head first into third just like Pete Rose. I'm going to be a hero. People will be talking about this for years to come. I'll show my dad that I am somebody and I can achieve.

Sure, the security guards will come after me, but I can duck 'em for a while. If I make it long enough, I may even land a spot on the blooper reel. Some of those guys are pretty big, though. Good thing I've had sixteen beers to numb the inevitable pain of being tackled by five gigantic men.

The fans need this, because this game sucks so bad. I am fully aware that the announcers will refer to me as "some idiot" for running onto the field, but I'm not trying to impress them. This is for the fans—for the city. I will have 50,000 strong rooting me on. Fathers and sons will be united in my cause. I am going to be an inspiration!

Okay, let me think. Do I need my shirt when I do this? Not really. Pants? Possibly, but wouldn't I have a better chance of being remembered if I'm only wearing my chones? I think so. Then it's settled. Just me and my skivvies. I wish I had thought of this sooner. I could have tattooed "goldenpalace.com" on my chest and made some cash to help post bail. Oh, well, can't live in the past—gotta be in the moment. Go time!

I'm over the railing. Oh shit, oh shit, oh shit. What am I doing? Fuck, here they come. Already? God dammit, I'll never make it to third. I'm in no-man's-land. Hey, is that an umpire? It is! He sucks! Fans hate umpires. I hate umpires. I am going to tackle that umpire.

Whoa, that's one big-ass security guard. Gotta change plans—cut right. Yes! My first ditch. I can hear the fans. I can hear them cheer. Whoop, missed me! I'm like Barry fucking Sanders. Can't catch me, no way. No one can catch me, no one can . . .

Aw, fuck, I'm down. Hey, don't hog-tie me, you assholes. I was only giving the people what they want. Ouch, my arm. Fucking pricks. Did I make it fifteen seconds? Ahh, get that nightstick off my neck. What are you . . .

Where the hell am I? Did I pass out? I must have. Wait a second. Oh, man, this is it. The stadium holding cell. Nice. I always knew I could make it here.

I wonder if the news is waiting outside to interview me. They probably are. I'm going to be famous. This is the smartest thing I have ever done. Everything went perfectly. I just wish I had managed to tackle that umpire. But that's okay. I'll get his ass next time!

Chapter Five

You Know What
I'm Doing Tonight

The World Is My Phone Booth!

What do you mean, "Shhhhhhh"? I'm the one that's on the phone. If anything, it's you who should be quiet, I can barely hear my friend Tucker with all of you jayholes scolding me all the time.

Yes, I know we're in a movie theater. I am not a moron. But we're only about twenty minutes into the film. Nothing happens in the first twenty minutes anyway—it's all character establishment.

Sorry, Tucker, you were talking about the new deck you're building on your ranch house . . .

HEY! Who threw that jujube at my head? I'm on the GD phone! You people are worse than those shushers I ran into at the library.

I am an important man who requires constant communication. There is no place too crowded or inconvenient for me to converse with my associates and friends about their lunch plans, sexual conquests, or graphically detailed medical problems. And that's something you'll all just have to deal with.

No, *you* shut the fuck up! This movie sucks anyway; I've already seen it. That guy kills the head of the drug cartel and then escapes by cutting off his face and wearing it out of the palace. It's hacky drivel. I don't even know why I'm here.

Hold on, Tucker, I want all the details on the length of the wood screws you're using. I'm just straightening something out here.

Hey, let me ask you people something. Was it the fifteen seconds that I took to answer my phone that pissed you all off? Because regardless of what you say, my ring tone is sweet. Everyone loves "The Thong Song." Sisqo is timeless. "Bumps like a truck . . . truck . . . truck . . ."

Take my phone outside? Why the hell would I want to do that? What's the point of having a cell phone if you can't use it everywhere? This is worse than my mother-in-law's wake last weekend. I got a high-priority call while I was on the kneeler in front of the casket. Brandon needed to know who I was starting at running back that week for my fantasy team. I'm only two games out of first. So I'll tell you what I told my father-in-law: chill the fuck out!

Oh, good, an usher. I'm glad you're here, young man. These people have been harassing me for the past twenty minutes, and I'm not going to stand for it anymore. Where are you taking me? To talk to a manager, I assume. An excellent idea. He'll straighten this out.

Tucker, I'm going to have to call you back. I'm about to see justice served. I'll call you as soon as I get on some form of crowded public transportation.

America Is for Americans

Y'all know that song that goes sumthin' like "this land is my land, this land is your land"? Well, they got half of it right. As for the second half, that's all bullshit. This land is my land, period. America is for Americans.

Folks try to come over here with those weird diseases, funny ways of talkin', and fascination with paved streets and think they can just take over my country? Not on my watch. And for the record, my watch also works underwater, up to three hundred feet deep. Notice I didn't say meters. That's an un-American measurement. But back to what I was talking about . . . What was I talking about? Oh, yeah: America. Land of the free, home of the brave, and not home to you, foreigner.

Did you know if it weren't for foreigners we wouldn't have terrorists? It's true. You can look it up. People from other countries have caused nothing but problems around here for years, and I aim to put a stop to it. I got a big sticker on the back of my truck that says "Stay Outta My Country"—that says it all. It's located in the coveted spot right next to my Tony Stewart sticker. And where do you think those stickers were manufactured? Right here in the good ol' USA. I don't never buy nuthin' made in China. Not now and not ever. And no matter how delicious people tell me they are, I will never be caught dead eating no egg roll. Same goes for rice.

And while we're talkin' about China, how 'bout them Indians? Not them Indians that we exterminated to get this land, but them dot-heads that you may remember from that Indiana Jones movie. I heard they got over a billion people there and now a bunch of 'em are tryin to come over here. No way, Jack—or Bakshi or whatever the hell weirdo name you got. I don't like talkin' to you when I call my credit card company, so I sure as shit don't want to talk to you face-to-face. Got that? You just stay over there and keep wiping your ass with your hand and we got no problems. Well, actually, *I* got no problems. You stand a very good chance of contracting cholera.

Here in America, we got rules. This ain't no Third World country where we go around shooting each other for nothing. Here we shoot people for two reasons: trespassing and fuckin' our wives. That's it. You wanna shoot people for not believing in Allah? Keep your ass in the desert, 'cause we've got no place for you here. And while you're out there in the middle of a sandstorm, dying of thirst and whacking off to a photo of a woman's calf, I'll be sitting on my couch, drinking Budweiser, eating an entire bucket of KFC, and watching the finest female bodies money can buy getting slammed by pros.

Anyhow, hopefully now you know that you're not welcome here. Look, I'm sorry that you've lost your home and all your possessions when your fragile government got overthrown by warlords, but I fail to see how that's my problem. Your country is in the midst of a terrible famine? Boo-hoo. You wanna hear about problems? Try payin' child support every month to some bitch that got knocked up on purpose, then ran off with your best friend. That's hardship.

And it ain't easy to come up with that money every month, seein' as how I got no job because your people swooped in here and took all the good ones. Given, I haven't been looking with much enthusiasm for a while now, but what's the point? They'd probably just find some Mexican to run the drill press for cheaper than what I'm willin' to, and I'd be out of work again.

So you deal with your shit and I'll deal with mine and we'll let the chips fall where they may from behind our respective borders. Have a nice life and better luck next time, ya stinkin' foreigner.

I'm, Like, Really into Philosophy

Oh, no, you didn't startle me! I was just checking out John's book collection. I guess you're taking a break from the party too. Let me just move over so you can get a better view of his CDs.

I think I recognize you. You're that girl who always sits in the back of the lecture hall in philosophy, aren't you?

Yeah, I'm, like, really into philosophy.

I love just, like, sitting around and thinking about heavy stuff, like "Why are we here?" and "How many stars are there?" and stuff. It's crazy. Like, we're so insignificant when you think about it, you know? I mean, you're not insignificant. Not to me. You're hot. But in the whole scheme of things.

Did you ever read *The Tao of Pooh*? That book changed my life. They made another one about Piglet.

I loved *The Matrix*. "There is no spoon. Woo woo woo . . ." Did you ever see the movie *Men in Black*? It will change your life. At the end, they do like this huge pullback, and it turns out that the whole galaxy is just part of an alien toy. Mind-blowing.

Do you know about phenomenology? It's like, everything isn't real, and it's just a phenomenon. So, like, this room wouldn't be real, John's hamper's not real. You're not real and I'm not real and we're not even really having this conversation. But we *are* having this conversation! And I'm real! So don't leave.

Everybody thinks philosophers are boring. But Nietzsche was hilarious! He had this great quote: "You go to a woman? Do not forget your whip!"

Yeah, you're right, women might not think that's so funny.

I'm studying to become a philotherapist. It's like a psychologist, but instead of prescribing pills you prescribe books. It's huge in Austin. Like, a guy would come in and he'd be all, "I'm sad," and so I'd write a prescription for *Zen and the Art of Motorcycle Maintenance* because I heard that's awesome. Haven't had a chance to tackle it yet myself, though.

You've got to listen to this song "What If God Was One of Us?" It's indie. It was by Joan Osborne. You might not recognize her, though, because she refused to appear on *The Osbournes.*

I get these amazing insights when I listen to Dream Theater.

What was my favorite philosophy book? It was called *The 20 Greatest Philosophers.* It was more of a magazine article than a book, though.

Taking off, huh? Yeah, I'm about to get back out there too. They're probably all like, "Where's Todd?" Well, it was good to see you. Maybe I'll see you in the lecture hall next week. Assuming there really is a lecture hall. "Woo woo woo . . ."

I'm Feeling Lucky Today

This is bullshit. I swear to God that Arab at the 7-Eleven is purposely giving me losers here. All I got so far is one goddamned free ticket. Seriously, I ain't never lost on four Spicy Cash Triplers in a row. I didn't know that was even possible. I mean, there's forty fuckin' boxes on the card. How can none of 'em match?

And I tell you what, I done scratched all the boxes on this Super Ca$hword, and I still don't know what that word is. Fuch . . . sia? Fuchsia? That ain't even a fucking word. I bitched at that clerk Jafar or Jizzmore or whatever the hell his name is and I said, "Hey, this ain't even a word." And that uppity Arab told me that it was a word. It's a color like pink. That's news to me.

And you know what's really burnin' my ass? I had a winner with that Find the 9's but I was scratching the sumbitch upside down. Before I figured it, I scratched the rest off to see where that other 9 was. They done that shit on purpose. If they made it find the 4's, nobody'd have that problem, but they don't wantcha to win. That's how they getcha.

You know which scratch-off I ain't playin' no more? Money Jar. Money Jar is a goddamned rip-off. Every time you scratch off three hammers, there is like two fuckin' dollars in the jar. All the ones with big dollar amounts don't got three hammers.

Look at this one: $50,000 Mania. Yeah, right. I bet you $50,000 that winning ticket never made it out the lottery office. Some Lotto fat cat's got that shit stashed away somewhere. I know that's what I'd do. It's all a fuckin' scam. Whole world's just a big scam job.

And it doesn't end with the lottery system. Everything's rigged. Remember when I was really into that Monopoly game at McDonald's? That was my passion. I must have eaten McDonald's five times a week during that whole goddamned promotion. But did I win a Jet Ski or that trunk full of real gold bars? No! And why? Because they set it up so that you can only get two properties and they don't release the third. So I'm sitting there with Ventnor and Atlantic Avenues and my thumb up my ass, with no Marvin Gardens to be found. Damn it!

I'm gonna try this Bee Lucky. Look at that bumblebee tryin' to fly off with the big ole money bag. That's funny. That fuckin' bee's stupid. He can't carry that money bag. That money bag prolly weighs thirty pounds. What would a bee want with all that money anyhow? All right, let's see what I got here . . . Now we're talking. Two hundred dollars. Hell yeah, another two hundred. Come on honeypot doubler. Honeypot doubler or another two hundred . . . Monkey-fuckin' son of a bitch! What do I have to do to goddamned catch a break around here?! I don't know how anybody gets ahead nowadays. I really don't.

Ah, well. I'm sure to win it all back when me and Roy head up to Atlantic City next weekend. Roy says craps is where the easy money is at, and he better be right, 'cause I just put a third mortgage on my house to fund the trip. I'm sure we'll come out on top. Roy has a system.

Captain's Log: Stardate 3272. Kirk Rocks!

November 21, 1986

Dear Captain Kirk (Mr. Shatner, ha-ha!),

You might remember me from the Pasadena Sci-Con last month. Stardate 4372.5! Just kidding! It was the 23rd. I was the Klingon/Romulan hybrid with both the forehead ridges AND the pointy ears. Of course they would never reproduce, because they are mortal enemies (which you know, but that is why I think my costume was the best). I should have won the costume contest (you saw it) but the judges must've been drunk on Romulan Ale. Ha-ha! (No, really.)

Anyway, I just wanted to write you and let you know that I'm not mad at you for the "autograph incident" Saturday night. I know a captain like you is really busy and popular and you have a lot of girlfriends. Even though it looked like you had plenty of time for the other fans, I understand that you couldn't talk to everyone, especially not a Klingon/Romulan (Klingulon?) like me. I would be pretty intimidated if I saw a six-foot-tall Klingulon in a dark alley, but hey, I don't know the Vulcan nerve pinch like our friend First Officer Nimoy does. Right? Right!

I can only assume you got my script notes and ideas outline for the next movie. I don't have a class-2 transporter, so I HAD to use the U.S. Mail. More like the U.S. Snail! Anyway, I'm sure your letter is on the way, warp speed ahead!

I do have a few questions:

1. In episode ten, when Dr. Korby put you on the spinning table to make an exact android copy of your body, were you dizzy afterward? Also, what happened to the android? Is it still around, or does Paramount have it? I bet it's worth a lot of money! I'd give forty quatloos for that thing!

2. Do you ever wish you could turn into the *Enterprise* (before it blew up, I mean)?

3. My friend Randy and I have a bet. How long can you hold your breath?

4. One more, Mr. Kirk. Is "The Star-Spangled Banner" different in Canada, or do they still sing it at all the ball games like we do here in the USA? Maybe at the next convention I'll enter the Alien Contest and dress up like a Canadian! HA-HA! Don't be mad.

I gotta get going. I've got to pick up my son and get to work in a half an hour. I'm not gonna tell you where I work (stranger), but let's put it this way, if your limo is ever in the drive-thru and you order a Big Hamburger and you hear "Qua'Plah!" you'll know it's me.

Live Long and Prosper!

Your friend (writing partner),
Glen Stevens

P.S. I know the Klingulon is my original idea, but you can go ahead and let Paramount use it if you want. I don't mind as long as it stays in the Federation! We don't want the Tholians to use it! (Ha-ha!) Or the Gorn!

I'm Just Like One of the Guys!

Hey, fellas! I know that this is supposed to be guys' night in, but I thought you might be willing to make an exception for little old me. After all, I'm totally just like one of the guys!

I can completely understand your wanting to exclude females from this gathering. They can be such a pain. They demand too much attention, they're annoying, and most are way too high maintenance. Not me. I'm different! I'm not all hung up on labeling a relationship. I'm up for whatever, whenever, wherever. High five!

Don't you hate it when girls are all hung up on what they look like? Not me. Check it out. Jeans and a tiny, tiny T-shirt. Baseball cap with a ponytail through the back. No makeup (except some mascara and lip gloss). If that doesn't make it clear that I'm just like one of the guys, I don't know what does.

Who's up for some chicken wings?

Hey, huddle up—guy talk for a sec. I just wanna just make one thing clear. This is definitely not a transparent ploy to gain your attention and affection. This is in no way some sad attempt to connect with you because it's the only way I know how.

Break!

Hey, can I be in your fantasy football league? I know I have no business being in it, but I'd love to loudly announce to the guys at work that I'm in a fantasy football league and constantly talk about how my players are performing even though I don't know what's going on and don't really care. Then they'd know for sure that I'm one of the guys! I think I'll draft Joe Montana with my first pick. Then I'll take LeBron James followed by Indiana Jones.

Hey, let's play Halo! I'm going to pick a character based on how cute his outfit is and then cheer loudly when something happens on the screen! I don't know what this game is all about, but I love competition, so bring it on! I'm gonna keep mashing all these buttons in hopes that something happens!

I have two brothers and we always wrestle. It's a guy thing.

Why, yes, that is a *Maxim* magazine on the back of my toilet next to my scented candles and decorative seashells. I have a subscription! That shit is funny, man! "Top Ten Reasons Why Sorority Girls Are Easy"? Oh my God, SO true!

I guess I've always just been a tomboy at heart. When all the other little girls in my neighborhood were playing with dolls, I was playing baseball with the boys. I was absolutely horrible and have never had any real interest in the sport, but I loved wearing pigtails and a cute jersey!

Wanna hear me burp the alphabet?

No, I totally don't mind if you ask my roommate out. But just between us dudes, she's a total slut and you probably wouldn't want anything to do with her. She doesn't even know when the Super Bowl is. I mean, come on. Hey, just looking out, bro.

Who's up for some tackle football?

Hey, Man, Check Out My Script

Excuse me, sir. I don't mean to bother you, but I love your work. I'm an aspiring screenwriter myself. Hey, you're looking pretty thirsty. Can I take your order, or are you still wrapping things up on your BlackBerry there? You are? Oh, well, no big rush. By the way, while I have you here, you should check out my script. I wrote it last year when I was waiting tables at Koi over in West Hollywood. I'm not going to be one of those no-talent ass-clowns who move here from Des Moines and write for *Gilmore Girls*.

Nope, not me. I'm keepin' it real. Oh, hey, did I tell you about my apartment over on Lanker-shim? It's pretty fuckin' sweet. Dude, there are so many hot chicks in my building! We're talking some serious talent here. They all know about my script. I won't let them read it, though, unless they bang me. That's how the game works, isn't it?

I'm going places.

On second thought, I don't think I will let you read my script. It's too good for a second-rate rate producer like you. No offense. This script makes *Good Will Hunting* look like a piece of toilet paper stuck to Ben Affleck's hairy ass. *Project Greenlight* can blow me. Bastards didn't like my script.

You don't want to read my script because Ben and Matt think I suck? I feel sorry for you, amigo. You'll wish I let you read it when you see me with Chloë Sevigny at Sundance next year, muggin' for the cameras. Yeah, that's right, biatch. Chloë Sevigny. She's so hot. I bet she'll like my script.

This baby's about to pop. I have a friend of a friend who knows someone's cousin who knows Tobey Maguire's agent's assistant. He says he might be able to get a copy of my script over to Tobey. But he's pretty busy now with the next Spiderman movie. I wonder who wrote that. Not really my kind of script, but we all have to make a buck, right?

So I suppose you want to know what my script is about. Okay. But first I'm going to have to get you to sign an NDA. What's that? You don't know what an NDA is? Neither do I. But my roommate who works in the mailroom over at Universal told me I'd better get people to sign one. Come to think of it, go to hell!

You aren't reading my script. What the hell was I thinking? This bad boy is for A-list eyes only.

Hey, did I tell you? My mom thinks my script is pretty cool. Her favorite movie is *Steel Magnolias.* She knows her shit, bro. She thinks I should get Tom Skerritt to play the lead. I'm thinking someone more like Jake Gyllenhaal. He'll keep it real. Just like he did in that one movie I saw. Maybe I'll get his sister too. She'll have to wait her turn in line, though. Chloë Sevigny gots first dibs on this badass mofo scriptwriter.

I'm thinking about writing another script. Just for insurance purposes. In case this masterpiece of mine doesn't win the Oscar. Never hurts to have options, especially in this town.

Speaking of options, I'm thinking about trading in my Jetta for a Toyota Prius. I heard Leonardo drives one of those things. Maybe I'll run into him while getting an oil change. He was pretty good in *Aviator.* That's the kind of raw intensity it's going to take to get a part in my film.

Oh, hey, did I tell you who I saw last Saturday over at Skybar? I saw that guy from *That '70s Show.* No, not that FES kid. Geez. The other one. That guy who was in the movie with Scarlett Johansen. Topher something. Yeah, he's cool. He told me I should send him a copy of my script. He forgot to give me his address, though.

Did I tell you how original this script is? I don't think anything has been done like it before. It'll blow your mind, bro.

Did I tell you about my boy Tate's new place up on Mulholland? His pad is off the hook, man. He has one of those infinity pools. I'm going to get me one of those after I make my first million. I bet Chloë Sevigny would like it. She can work on her tan while she sips Cristal out by the pool. I'll have plenty of that shit once I sell this fucker.

So anyway, I'll let you read my script if you really want to. It's going to be the next big thing, man. You'll really thank me for it when you're done. This thing is going to be huge. You heard it from me first.

No! I won't give you a Venti for the price of a Tall. My manager might find out, and then I'll get fired and he won't read my script. I heard his neighbor's uncle is that guy from *Sideways.* He'll for sure like my script.

My Script Spoilers

Spoiler 1

The main character, a brilliant but underachieving and underappreciated screenwriter who waits tables for a living, is actually based on me!

Spoiler 2

The character "Jeff" is based on the good-looking bartender who stole my girlfriend. He dies within the first five minutes.

Spoiler 3

Throughout the film, you'll notice several homages to fellow screenwriters Quentin Tarantino, Kevin Smith, and Wes Anderson. And by "homages," I mean blatant thefts.

Spoiler 4

The part of "Jerome" was originally written for the versatile character actor Philip Seymour Hoffman, but due to scheduling conflicts it will probably be played by my fellow waitstaff member Tyler.

Spoiler 5

My movie blows.

Turn Signals Are a Waste of My Time

This lane sucks. It's so boring. I hate this lane and I'm going to get out of it.

I suppose I could use my turn signal to make those around me aware of my decision. But that would involve reaching all the way up there and grabbing that thing. And then I'd have to remember which way to move it to indicate the direction that I plan on veering my car. And quite frankly, I'm not even certain of that yet. That's going to be a game-time decision. Then after my move I'd have to put the thingee back to where it was so that people would know I'm done changing lanes. It all sounds like a big hassle. I think I'll just skip it and make my move. Here we go.

Well, that guy wasn't happy. I'm probably not on his Christmas list anymore. But how was I supposed to know that his car was exactly parallel to mine in the lane I was pulling into? I suppose I could have looked, but where's the adventure in that? Life is a game, people, and I came to play. Side-view mirrors can be reattached and those sidewipe marks can be buffed out, but you know what you can't purchase at the Auto Zone? Memories.

I'm bored again. I don't like this lane anymore. Think I'll mosey back over to my previous lane. I'll just ease her in here . . .

Whoa. I hear ya, buddy, your horn works just fine. Kudos to your horn. I'll admit, that was a rather abrupt move on my part. And true, you didn't have much of a heads-up, because once again I chose not to signal. And yes, I can clearly see that you have children in your car, so you can stop pointing at them. It's pretty hard to miss them in those car seats. But I like to think that they just learned a valuable lesson, compliments of me. Be aware. Keep your guard up. Because you never know when life might throw you a curveball. Thus endeth the lesson. You're welcome.

Oh, man, I just realized that I haven't looked at the road in more than forty-five seconds. That's something. You might think that would be my record, but you'd be wrong. I once went about three minutes without watching the road. It wasn't even intentional. I was just fiddling with the radio, text-messaging some friends, and reading an *Entertainment Weekly* when I realized that I had just broken my previous record of two minutes and thirty seconds. I ended up crashing my car into a Walgreens. The management was none too happy, but it's cool. I'm insured.

Think I'll tap my brakes a few times for no real reason. I just like the way the red looks reflected on the front of your car.

Boy, you sure are upset, aren't you? I'd probably hear your screams if I didn't have this top-forty radio station blasting. Your face is as red as a beet. Your anger would probably be comical to me if I took the time to think about it, but as it is I'm busy adjusting my air-conditioning vents. I just cannot seem to get the temp right in here. Sometimes it's too cold, and then I get hot.

Hey, looks like my exit is coming up. It's way up ahead there. I suppose I'd have plenty of time to signal, but I think we both know where this is going. I'll slam on my brakes just as we're passing up the ramp, overshoot it by about fifteen feet, throw it in reverse, and back her up. I love the open road.

Pot Really Opens My Mind

Pot is the best. Seriously, man, it is. I swear. It totally opens up portals of my mind that I never knew were there. It's crazy. And then when it wears off it's, like, gone. Then I smoke some more and it comes back. Like I said, crazy.

You've never smoked pot before? You're probably wondering what I'm talking about, huh? Well, let me let you in on a little secret—pot totally opens your mind to new ways of thinking. It will change your whole view on life, man. Trust me.

Take for example the time I realized that even though they say the world is round, it isn't. Think about it, man, there are mountains and valleys and shit. How could it really be round? I mean, it's sort of round, but technically it really isn't. You think I could have come up with that shit if I weren't high? No way, man, not even close.

I've even figured things out about myself when I was high that I never would have without my lady Mary Jane. She's like my shrink, man. For instance, I've been thinking that I should be more relaxed when things don't go my way. This world is tough, man, and we're all uptight, but what good is it doing us, all this stress? All it's gonna get us is an early grave. We gotta be mellow, man, and not just personally but as a society. Think about that for a minute.

Oh, and you know what else? I'm funny as hell when I'm high. Seriously, I thought of this one joke the other night that had me cracking up! I'd tell you what it was, but I kinda forgot it. It was something about a weather balloon or some shit, but trust me, it was funny. I was rolling.

Let's see, what else? There's so many awesome ways that pot has changed me. I mean, I used to be a total nerd before, you know? I bought all that shit they fed us about pot being a "gateway drug" and the root of all evil. What a load that was. Pot is the best. I even smoke it in the morning when I get out of bed. How cool is that?

By the way, did you see that movie *Being John Malkovich*? I'll bet the guy who wrote that was totally smoking pot. That shit was crazy. The first time I saw that

Pot Really Opens My Mind

I was way stoned and it blew my fucking mind. Now I pretend to be inside different people's heads and it totally trips me out, even when I'm not high. All this thanks to pot.

You get how this works? Let me tell you—if this doesn't make you want to smoke like I smoke, then there must be something wrong with you. Your small and simple world might seem safe to you, but you're missing out, man.

You don't want any? Too heavy for you? Fine then, more for me. I'm outta here. Have fun in Squaresville, pal! I'll be on the flip side, expanding my mind, and you'll still be here with your, your . . . normal-size mind, getting stupider. Your call. Okay, fine, then. Later days, dude, later days.

We Own This Battle of the Bands

Man, this is gonna be great. I have no doubt in my mind that this show will be packed. I sent out five different e-mails to everyone in my address book, so I've done everything I can on this end. I bet that guy from Atlantic Records will come too. I'm sure he got our demo. I sent four copies to his office, two to his house, and I put one on his porch. We are so in. My guitar solo on "Never the Last Time Since the First Time I Saw You (Making Hard Love)" probably blew him away. I bet he couldn't even handle the sweet riffage on that bad boy.

Is my hair right? I better break out the Aqua Net and get these locks teased just right. I don't want to disappoint any of the ladies out there. My future fans will be heartbroken if I'm not at the peak of my sexiness. With these leather pants I'll be surprised if they even notice my hair. My ass looks so good in these. Maybe this tank top is too Creed. I should rock the leopard print, short-sleeve button-up. Open three buttons so the ladies can see all that manly chest hair and my gold cross. Chicks love the cross. It says, "He'll fuck me all night but then he'll take me home to meet his parents." Who would have guessed that this small representation of the Savior dying for our sins could be such a hot accessory? Thanks, JC.

Shit, they're ready. Where's my Gibson? Did I change the strings already? There she is. My beautiful Betty. Oh yeah, Betty, you like it when I stroke you, don't you, baby? You're gonna play good for Daddy tonight, aren't you? I promise I won't smash you like I did Veronica.

Fuck me. Is Terry wearing leather pants too? That asshole! I told him I was wearing leather tonight. We're gonna look like some kind of faggoty boy band now. Shit, they want us to get on stage. Here we go.

Let's say a prayer, guys. Huddle up. Dear God, thank you for giving us another chance to rock the panties off all the little girls. Lord, we know that you're pretty busy with all the famine, war, and disease in the world, but please make sure we have a killer show and destroy all these other pussy bands, because you know we paid a lot to play here tonight. In Jesus Christ's name we pray. Let's rock!

God damn, these lights are bright. I can't see shit. But at least I know all the hot chicks can see me. Should I do a jump-kick at the chorus? Terry did it the last time. But I fucking bitched him out for it, so he'll know better this time. Two more bars. Now! Yeah, I'm flying! Shit! That landing fucking hurt. Am I still plugged in? Damn it! Terry jumped at the same time. Now everyone's gonna think we're doing choreography or something. This is bullshit. That guy is a shitty lead singer anyway. This is a rock band. Doesn't he know everyone comes for the guitar player?

Jesus, is Terry doing the humping-the-scarves-on-his-mike-stand thing? That is so tired. Now he's leaning back to back with our new bass player and singing! Fuck that. That new guy is singing my harmony! What the balls? I'll show those fuckers. My guitar solo is gonna blow everyone away.

Oh, yeah. That chick is totally looking at me. I like the way she's got her bangs teased. That's almost the same way I do it. Oh, damn. That's my brother. Too many dudes with long hair in here. But that chick next to him IS definitely looking at me. She knows I'm on fire. I bet it's the cross. Little church girl wants to grab my naughty ax, doesn't she? Flash me, you sexy bitch. What, no flash for Daddy? Maybe if I put my foot on the monitor and shake my hair back and forth she'll show me some skin. Shit, did I just knock over my beer? Sweet, it spilled right on her. Maybe now she'll take that shirt off. Damn, she's hot. I wonder if she's gonna be backstage after the show.

Oh, it's almost time for my solo. Fuck, what key is this song in? Like it matters. I'm gonna play so fast, these people won't know what hit 'em. Should I slide across the stage on my knees? Or should I just collapse in a heap? Yeah, that always slays them. Ouch. That fucking hurt. I should've worn my knee brace. Damn. I think that was the wrong note. I hope no one noticed. I better do it again so they think it was intentional. Fuck, yeah. Eddie Van Halen is my bitch.

That was the tastiest solo ever! Now if Terry could just hurry up with the big ending so I can hear my fucking applause. Let me shred another really long riff after everyone stops just to put some sauce on that shit. Damn, I'm good. Where's the applause? Maybe I just can't hear it because I'm so close to the amp.

Sweet, the houselights are coming up. What the fuck? There are only, like, twenty people here! I told Terry we should have put some flyers at that Chipotle by the college. Now we're not even gonna get free drinks.

Man, I wish that chick in the stonewashed jeans were flashing me. She looks like she's probably only had one or two kids.

Why's everyone booing? Terry sucks but his voice isn't that awful. I'd better play something solo to win this crowd back. I think it's time to get The Led out.

I Have Amazing Taste in Music

So you got the new Shins CD, huh? Oh yeah? Do you like it? You do? That's cool. No, I'm glad you like it. It's just not really my thing, is all. Sure, I like the Shins. Or I used to. I'm just not a big fan of the stuff they've been putting out lately. See, I was a fan of theirs before they became mainstream.

Now, their earlier stuff, that's where it's at. Do you have their first album, *Oh, Inverted World*? You don't? Oh, man, you don't know what you're missing.

In my opinion they really produced their best stuff before they even became the Shins.

Their original band, Flake, was so much more raw and real. They're too overproduced today. They've become very commercialized.

Actually, if you want a truly pure Shins experience, I have a bootleg of a VHS tape of their lead singer, James Mercer, playing an acoustic version of "Smells Like Teen Spirit" at his high school talent show in 1994.

That's the problem with people. They only like what they can hear on the radio. No one wants to work for their music anymore. They have to be told what to like and have it drilled into their heads by the powers that be again and again.

Personally, I haven't listened to the radio in fifteen years. If you have ever heard a band on the radio, then I can assure you I am not a fan.

Anyone can like music that's enjoyable to listen to. Where's the challenge in that?

U2? Yeah. I guess they're okay. But for my money they should have just hung it up after *Joshua Tree*. All they've been producing since then is sound tracks for Pepsi and Chevrolet commercials. And yes, they'll make it into the Rock and Roll Hall of Fame. Whatever that means.

And it's totally my right to judge U2 and speak harshly of them. This despite the fact that I play no instruments and don't possess a creative bone in my frail, cadaverous body.

The Beatles? Not a big fan. I know that's not going to win me any popularity contests, but then I've never been concerned with what's popular. Just what's good.

117

I will say that I was a big fan of their pre-Beatle work as the Quarry Men. Without Ringo in there to muck up the beat, they were actually quite enjoyable for a brief time.

I have a bootleg of them playing at the Cavern in Liverpool in 1958, and the quality is so bad that it's essentially inaudible. That was the only thing I listened to for an entire year.

Bob Dylan? Sure, he used to be good before he sold out and got all commercial in 1960. The only good stuff that he ever produced was the music he performed in Greenwich Village before he actually began recording anything. And no, I obviously can't claim to have technically "heard" his music from that period, but it has been described to me in great detail, and I assure you that from what I understand it far surpasses any of his subsequent work.

I stopped listening to American music about ten years ago.

For a while, I was listening only to German techno, twenty-four hours a day. There's something so simplistically complicated about it! The constant, driving mechanical beats and German profanity that emanated from my apartment day in and day out did not win me any Best Neighbor awards. I told them I was sorry that I wasn't blaring Maroon 5 out of my apartment but that I would not succumb to their musical ignorance. The situation escalated until a surly mob gathered outside my apartment one night. Threats were issued, compromises were made.

It was at this point that my musical interests turned to Asia. The continent, that is. I'm particularly fond of a Pakistani brother/sister folk duo called Urdu and Shia. Talk about raw! Urdu plays a lutelike instrument that he made himself with fish bones and dried strips of goat hide. Shia sings and plays a drum made from a gourd that was originally part of her mother's dowry but was passed to Shia when her mother died of dysentery. Now that's music!

I switched it up last year and started solely listening to Gregorian chant. I preferred the ninth-century chants popularized by Guido of Arezzo, but I was no stranger to the work of the Medieval Byzantines. But as I became more educated I realized that even Gregorian chant had become tainted by commercialism, with its *Time-Life Christmas Collection* and all. It was not, in fact, the purest form of music.

The only thing that I will listen to now is wind chimes. And not on a crazy-windy day when they're going all apeshit. Only when it's balmy.

So enjoy that Shins album, with its melodic hooks and chirpy beats, simpleton. If you need me, I'll be out on the front porch, waiting for a slight breeze.

Damn, My Pencil-Thin Beard Is Perfect!

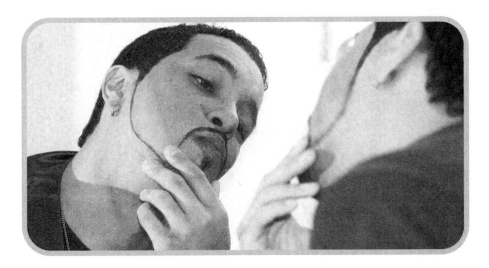

YES! Three years of pimping this short, superthin beard, and finally it is perfect. I gotta take a picture of this. Holy shit, there's an area on my jawline where the beard is down to a single hair across, and it is mirrored exactly on the other side. Fantastic!

Chicks dig precision.

I should have been a heart surgeon. Those rich assholes have no idea when I deliver their pizza that I could have been the best surgeon in the world. It takes a still hand to shave such a thin line. I wonder why more doctors don't go for this look. Probably against dress code. Besides, all the women patients would be walking around all moist and shit if the doctors looked like this.

Damn, even the subtly curved tapering of my sideburns is perfect. I bet no one has ever had a beard this perfectly symmetrical—not even that A.J. jerkoff from the Backstreet Boys. And screw that guy, anyway. I wanted to have a really thin beard way before he and that band of turd burglars got popular.

I can't believe I almost gave up and shaved this thing off last month. I thought those two hairs that connect my tiny mustache to the wispy edges of my perfectly shaped "chin strap" would never grow in. But now here they are, in all their glory. And it's not gross at all.

It's too bad I have to work tonight. I'd have my pick of the chicks at the club with this exquisite thing on my face. I should call off. I bet Caitlin will be at Cloud with her slutty friends. There's no way she can resist me like this.

Damn, My Pencil-Thin Beard Is Perfect!

Fuck it. I'm calling off.

God dammit! I wish there were a way to make my hair stop growing . . . That's the tragedy of this whole situation. Tomorrow my perfectly shaped, pencil-thin beard will be gone—consumed by a day of growth. It's kinda like a beautiful sunset in that way: amazing in the moment, but too perfect to last.

Ah, well, I'll always have today . . . and that picture. I should drop this off at a one-hour photo just in case. I really need to get a digital camera.

All right, beard, let's go get some sleeve.

These Personalized License Plates Should Get the Word Out That I'm a Huge Douchebag

They finally came. I had heard that it takes a little while longer to have personalized license plates made, I just didn't expect it to take two whole weeks. But all good things are worth waiting for. I mean, what fun would Christmas be without all that buildup?

Regardless, I'd better get out to the garage and get these babies rigged up. How else are my fellow motorists going to know that I'm a huge douchebag?

Honey! Have you seen my Phillips screwdriver? My new plates just came and I want to get them on the Stratus ASAP so that I can start spreading the word about what a massive hand job I am! Shake a leg! Every second counts!

Boy, they look even better than I imagined. I had tried to create a mental image of what they were going to look like several times since that trip to the DMV, but nothing can compare to actually seeing them right here in all their glory, with the official logos and insignias on them and whatnot.

This is truly a momentous event in my tragically empty life.

It's kind of funny to think that there are actually people out there who are driving around with nonpersonalized license plates. What a golden opportunity to express themselves, missed! I mean, here they have this empty canvas on which to paint a message for the world that encapsulates what they are in a combination of ten numbers and letters, and they're missing it!

It's their loss.

Does it cost a little extra? Sure. But the finer things always do, don't they? An extra fifty dollars a year is a small price to pay for turnpike infamy.

You can only imagine my disappointment when I was informed by the DMV lady that someone had already laid claim to my plate of choice: LUVS2GOLF. But in retrospect, I suppose it was wishful thinking to assume that no other avid linksman would have snapped that one up. I tried a few variations on my theme, but both RTHRBGLFNG and LETSGOLF4 were taken as well.

I started to get really frustrated. Without those plates, how was I supposed to inform all of Interstate 76 that I'm an enormous cock-gobbler who enjoys swinging the old nine iron when I get the chance? What are people supposed to do? Guess?

It was at this point that I made the difficult decision to completely change direction and advertise one of my many other interests with my license plates. For instance, it's no big secret that I am a rabid Ohio State fan. Because despite my never having attended that or any university, I have lived in Ohio my entire life. So with that in mind, I tried GOBUCKSGO, BUCKFAN1, and OSTATEGO. Unfortunately, all these second-tier but completely respectable plates had been commandeered by my fellow Buckeyes fans. I can't begrudge them that either. They just wanted it more.

In the end, I settled on GONFSHIN. This was a real compromise on my part because I am not what anyone would consider to be an avid fisherman. In truth, I'm lucky to get out to the lake once or twice a season. But I was simply running out of hobbies to pronounce with my license plates, and desperate times call for desperate measures. Maybe I'll start fishing more now that it is expected of me. I don't have any problem with that.

But the literal message of my personalized license plates is really secondary to what they say symbolically. When people see those little beauties they will indeed assume that I am a spirited angler, but there will also be nary a shadow of a doubt that the man behind the wheel of my car is a Grade-A fuckstick. Mission accomplished.

I LUV VNTY PLTS

Chapter Six

No, Dude, I Have to Work

This Office Snack Situation Is Unacceptable

Memo

TO: SHDB Personnel
FROM: Bonnie McPherson, Office Manager
SUBJECT: Office Snacks
DATE: 11/27/2006

It has recently come to my attention that certain people have been abusing the free snacks we provide in the company break room. Specifically, there have been reports of individuals raiding the snack cupboards as soon as a new shipment arrives, then hoarding whole boxes or cases of a particular snack in or around their personal work space, as to ensure that nobody else shares or enjoys their chosen snacks. There have even been allegations of people taking snacks off the premises to share with their families and roommates.

Now, I think we can all agree that I am not a demanding person. When I volunteered to take on the job of office coordinator in addition to my regular duties with no pay increase whatsoever, I did so not because I desperately crave power and authority, as many of you seem to believe (I overhear things), but because I want our office to run in a smooth and efficient manner.

That being said, let it be understood, right here and now, that ANYONE caught stashing or stealing string cheese, gummy fruits, pretzels, or any other company-provided snacks will be written up, with a permanent report in his or her Human Resources file. I am not just whistling Dixie here, people.

We provide these snacks for you free of charge, as a way of saying thank you for your hard work and dedication. However, if you people cannot be adult enough to share and enjoy the snacks responsibly, certain preventative measures will be taken to stop the rogue snack pilferers who are selfishly determined to ruin a good thing for the rest of us.

If the snack theft does not stop immediately, I will have no choice but to put locks on all snack cabinets, then ration out a prudent daily amount of said snacks for employees to enjoy. I'm not yet sure what these rations will be, but I can assure you that our overall snack consumption will decrease dramatically, resulting in a break room climate of post-apocalyptic desperation for the few scraps of food I decide to make available. It will be like *Lord of the Flies* every single day, all in the quest of a small pouch of Wheat Thins. If for some reason the rationing doesn't work and people continue to find ways to abuse the snacks, we will cease offering them altogether. Then you will all starve or, worse, be forced to purchase your own food.

Also, while we are on the topic of break room indulgence, I would like to remind everyone—once again—that the FIJI waters located on the top shelves in the refrigerator are reserved for consumption by upper management only. These are executive waters. All other employees should be drinking the Arrowhead water provided on the lower shelves of the fridge, or drawing water from the fountain in the hallway. If you keep working hard and paying your dues, one day you too could be enjoying the cool, crisp waters of the executives. If you already are, rest assured that we will find out who you are soon enough, and, mark my words, you will never enjoy these waters again.

If you have witnessed anyone abusing the snack situation or undeservedly partaking in the executive waters, please do not hesitate to notify a superior. Even if you're just suspicious someone might be getting more snacks than yourself, it never hurts to report them to either myself or the proper management figures. Unless those people abusing the snacks are themselves management figures, in which case you are encouraged to file an anonymous report with upper management, in which case one of the executives will investigate the matter, especially if it involves their water.

Let's hope that I don't have to address this situation again.

Bonnie

This Week Is Going to Be Brutal

MONDAY
- Send the e-mail forward "You know your job sucks when . . ." to everyone in the office.
- Tell everyone that I saw Sharon get hammered at TGI Friday's even though she promised she was only going to stay "for one more daiquiri."
- Tell the new temp how weird everyone else is: "Fred is crazy about apples," "Karen and Danny are having an affair in the copy room," and "The janitor pisses in the coffeepot."
- Kiss the boss's ass and ask him his weekend golf score. Possible responses:
  1. "Oh, you'll hit 'em better next weekend."
  2. "Wooo—Tiger Woods better be looking over his shoulder!"
  3. "Better not let the wife know she has a professional golfer in the house! She'll want a bigger allowance!"
  (use best judgment)

TUESDAY
- Tell Sharon that I have no idea why everyone in the office thinks she got drunk and went home with a TGI Friday's busboy. Say something like, "Were you drunk? I couldn't even tell."
- Deny sending the e-mail forward "You know your job sucks when . . ." when the boss brings it to my attention. Say, "The janitor is trying to get back at me because I caught him pissing in the coffeepot."
- Sneak on to Fred's computer and put the screensaver of the cartoon man having sex with an apple on it, because everyone knows how crazy he is about apples.

WEDNESDAY
- Watch through the front office window as the janitor takes his walk of shame out of the building after being fired for pissing in the coffeepot. Make sure everyone in the office is aware that it was me that tipped off the boss.
- Piss in the coffeepot.
- Tell Fred it was that new temp that changed his screensaver. Say, "Yeah, I don't know what the fuck is up with that guy."
- Tell the temp that Fred just doesn't like him for some reason so he better steer clear. Say, "Yeah, Fred's like that. Total dickhead. I think it's got something to do with all those apples he eats."
- Enter copy room. Attempt to copy my taint without anyone seeing.

THURSDAY

- Buy ice to make the swelling in my right eye go down.
- Write memo to the office stating that Danny's punching me for "spreading the rumor that he and Karen are having an affair" was totally out of line. His wife kicking him out was no fault of mine.
- Accept the boss's invitation to play golf this weekend and offer to pay for it.
- Send Danny's wife another anonymous note stating that whatever she does, she should not let Danny back in the house. Make him rot in a cheap hotel.
- Make second attempt at copying my taint, this time with a piece of tinfoil covering my balls and ass. Misty said the copy machine's laser may give me testicle or colon cancer.
- Lock door so Misty doesn't walk in on me again.

FRIDAY

- Ask Danny's wife out on a date.
- Ask Misty out. She's already seen me straddling a copy machine and didn't seem too freaked out.
- Throw an apple over Fred's cubicle, duck, and run away. Later, blame the temp.
- Tell the boss that I can't play golf with him because I have to help Danny move the stuff out of his house. Make sure to be convincing; he may be catching on that I don't even play golf.
- Avoid Danny!
- When leaving work, run quickly by the taco vending stand that the former janitor and his family have set up outside the building to make a living. TGIF!

I Am Perfect for This Job

Thank you. I appreciate the opportunity to interview here. I really admire this firm, as well as the values it represents. And I believe I would be a really great addition to your culture of leadership. No, I don't know anybody who works here, but I still feel I "get" this place. I've read your whole Web site.

Why do I think I'd be a good fit here? Well, because you're a firm of leaders, and I was a leader in school. I was elected to the undergraduate student government two years in a row. Well, actually, the first year I wasn't elected, I was appointed. You see, our government was modeled after the six branches of the United Nations. It's a little hard to explain, but if you'd like me to draw a diagram . . . no? Okay.

I see that you have my résumé there. Not to pat myself on the back, but I think you'll see that my accomplishments speak for themselves.

What position did I play on the varsity baseball team? Out of curiosity, why do you ask? Oh, you roomed with Coach Stennis when you went to school! Small world! Yeah, did I write "varsity" on there? That's a typo. I played coed intramural softball. Let me just fix that on your copy . . .

What's that? Sure, you can call the references I've listed. Oh, but not the first one. I meant to take that guy off there! Here, let me just help you scratch that off . . .

My GPA? Well, there's a funny story about my GPA. My junior year, I got into some academic problems. Totally out of my hands. Apparently some members of the faculty didn't take too kindly to my editorials denouncing them for their complicity in that kid's burning death in his dorm. And that had an impact on my GPA. But from that I learned more lessons about leadership.

An experience in which I overcame a challenge? One thing comes to mind. It involved this guy named Carl Drake. Just a terrible person. A real sicko. Took pleasure in others' misery. He caused me all sorts of trouble that year. He was always . . .

Oh, you know Carl Drake? He's interning here? Son of the regional senior manager?

Well, once again, small world. Boy, I am not going to play the lotto tonight.

No, I don't remember the rest of the story. Never mind.

Travel? Oh, I'm prepared to travel. I understand you have a lot of agricultural clients in the Fresno market. I figure this is a good time to see the world, before I get tied down. Are you married?

Oh, separated—I see. I'm sorry. Well, you're a young man. This is a good time to get that out of the way before you get burdened with kids. They call those "starter marriages."

Oh, you have two kids? Wow. Congratulations. Children are such a blessing.

One of my most marketable qualities is that I can really read people. For example, I can tell by the way you keep staring at your watch and not making eye contact with me that we're about done here.

Before I go, could I have a business card? No? Okay. Well, in that case, is there any chance that I could have that copy of my résumé back? I assume that you won't be needing it, and that's my last copy.

That's not really necessary—I think I can remember where the parking garage is, but if you'd feel more comfortable having someone personally escort me out, sure!

Oh—hi, Carl.

October 26, 2006

Human Resources Manager
Quicken Loans Arena
One Center Court
Cleveland, OH 44115

Dear Sir or Madam:

I am writing to request an interview with your company. I'll jump-start the interview now:

What is the greatest asset I have to offer an employer?

I am a tireless worker with his eye on the prize. If I have a weakness, it's that I never save enough time for myself because I love working so much.

Why am I seeking a new position?

Since receiving my honorable discharge from the U.S. Army for suffering injuries while fighting for our freedom in Iraq, I now desire to get back to where I belong, the business-guy world.

Where do I see myself in five years?

In my office at your company, working quietly and diligently.

Sincerely,

Michael J. Martone
Businessman

fax to Kinkos • e-mail lovestowork@hotmail.com
32145 Main Street • Cleveland, OH 44444 • Phone (216) 555–8764

MICHAEL J. MARTONE

Objective   Ideal position would be businessman, with $18,000 to $250,000 in salary with benefits and the following additional compensation: corner office, receptionist, stocks and bonds, commemorative coins.

Experience   **1996–present:**   Business Incorporated,   *Cleveland, OH*
Vice President of Impressive Business Dealings
• Outsourcing and inbuying
• Overseeing important industry
• Burning the midnight oil

1992–1995:   The Newspaper,   *Cleveland, OH*
Reporter
• Wrote lots of articles
• Took excellent photographs
• Won Puletsur Prize and donated it to charity

Additional   General life experience, fiber optics, PowerPoint, acting Commishioner
Experience   of fantasy football league.

Education   Yale
Harvard
Oxford
DeVry
Hold degrees in Business Running and Profit Making

Interests   Work, putting in overtime, not drinking, smoking, or doing anything else that would increase the company's health-care costs. I do enjoy reading business magazines and upselling.

REFERENCES UNAVAILABLE
BECAUSE THEY WERE ALL BURNED UP IN A FIRE

fax to Kinkos • e-mail lovestowork@hotmail.com
32145 Main Street • Cleveland, OH 44444 • Phone (216) 555–8764

Memo

TO: SHDB Personnel
FROM: Bonnie McPherson, Office Manager
SUBJECT: GREAT to be back
DATE: 12/11/2006

Hello, everyone,

It is so good to be back! Thank you all for the cards and kind wishes. I could feel your prayers coming to me there in my bed! The doctor says that he hadn't ever seen hemorrhoids that bad. But as long as I use my seat pillow and my cane, I should be back to 100 percent in no time. (Just be careful . . . that's not hand lotion in my cube.)

First off, I want to say thank you, thank you, THANK YOU to Jenny Wilson, our beloved receptionist, for helping out with the office manager duties while I was out. While not everything was done exactly the way I would have done it, Jenny doesn't have thirty-seven years of experience with it like I do. Let's give her a big SHDB round of applause. Remember, everyone's a flower waiting to be showered with praise and have smiles shine on them, so they can open up and be as beautiful as they can be!

One quick thing I would like to bring up: my singing flower seems to have disappeared from my desk while I was gone. The one that would sing "Here Comes the Sun" every time someone walked by? I know it has soul, but I'm pretty sure it doesn't have legs! I understand that someone must have thought it wasn't bringing me any happiness while I was out, but if they could please return it, it would be much appreciated. If you want to get your own, I got it at Spencer's . . . maybe you'll even get one as your Secret Santa gift this year.

I noticed a few other things seemed to have happened while I was out. First off: binder clips. Binder clips are free for the taking from the supply closet, and I would like to keep it that way, but we all have to play as a team for that to happen. For starters, there are different sizes of binder clips, and these are appropriate for different sizes of jobs. Please do not use the half-inch binder clips for only a few pieces of paper. An eighth-inch binder clip would be completely satisfactory and save everyone a bunch of trouble. Also, please make sure to mark how many of which size of binder clip you are taking on the acquisitions sheet on the inside of the supply closet door, and date and initial it. This way we can track when we need to order more, so everyone always has an adequate supply. I know there was some grumbling when the procedure for acquiring binder clips was submitting a written request to me, so in order to avoid going back to that, let's all make a concerted effort to work within the rules. I know we can do it.

I would also like to address what's been happening with staplers. As noted in my memo of July 24, 2004, staplers are assigned to managers only. If any non-manager needs to use a stapler, that person is free to either use it in a manager's office or use the group stapler, which is attached to the supply closet. However, lately I have noticed staplers appearing in the cubicles of several non-managers. I work very hard to maintain my spreadsheet of stapler locations, and if I don't know where the staplers are at all times, it makes my job much more difficult. So please, only use the staplers in the managers' offices, or at the supply closet. Think of staplers like real estate: the most important thing is location.

The coffee station has been a disaster lately. Remember, everybody: your cup, but everybody's mess. If we all just make sure to clean up those Splenda packets, spilled coffee grounds, and dripped cream, everyone will have a more pleasant coffee station experience. The word on the street is that the folks down at Crapient had to switch to a coin-operated coffee machine because they couldn't handle the responsibility of a full coffee station, and I know we don't want that here.

Finally, I have noticed that we have been going through toilet paper at an alarming rate. Remember our bathroom saying: a pair of squares is more than fair. There was an awful lot of discussion about switching from the bargain basement toilet paper to the softer brand we're using now, and to make it happen I had to promise that they would actually save money because people would use less. But I swear, some of you must be making yourselves pillows with the stuff, we're flying through it so fast. If everyone just adopts a policy of folding to find a clean spot (remember: creasing, not increasing), we can all avoid moving back to Sandpaper Land.

Again, everyone, thank you guys so much for your kind thoughts and prayers while I was out, and I am so happy to be back. We are going to make this next year better than ever here at SHDB, and I can't wait!

Big hugs,
Bonnie

I Am the Greatest Pretend Worker This Company Has

Hi. I'm a thirty-year-old computer technician living in Chicago, Illinois. I can't tell you where I work, but let's just say my company's initials are AT&T. I've been working at their corporate headquarters as a help desk computer technician for three years now, and I can honestly tell you that I haven't done an ounce of work since I've been here. Not one.

"How does he do it?" you must wonder. The answer is simple. I slack off with precision. You see, efficient slacking requires a high degree of focus, detail, and commitment. Contrary to what you might believe, slacking takes discipline. Here are some tips that will help ensure that you need never do actual work again.

1: Always Look Frustrated

Nothing says, "I'm working hard" like a constant pained expression on your face. It should be almost as if your face is saying, "Man, I need another cup of coffee—it's the only thing that will help me get through all this work I'm doing"; it doesn't matter that you're reading about Barry Bonds's increasing hat size on ESPN.com. Look as though you are going through utter hell. It won't feel natural at first, but eventually the muscles in your face will conform to the look, as mine did long ago. And then it's smooth sailing.

When someone walks by, say something like "Phew! Will this day ever end?" Or "Man, I could go for an Applebee's riblet platter about now!" If he suddenly wants to go to Applebee's with you, look at him as if he is crazy and say, "Yeah, maybe in a dream world, but some of us have work to do."

2: Walk Fast

A man who walks with a purpose instills confidence in those around him without saying a single word. So even though it requires more energy, it's better to look as if you're in a hurry no matter where you're going. Don't be afraid to take a few extra trips around the office so everyone knows you are the guy that's "gotta get the job done!" even though you're really going to the bathroom to look at the September issue of *Jugasaur* for the fourth time today.

3: Always Have Stuff in Your Hands

Any time anyone sees you, make sure you are holding something work related. I don't care what it is. If you want people to think you are busy, make your hands look busy. People who have stuff in their hands must be doing something work related. I mean, why would anyone walk around the office with an empty manila folder just to sit back down again? I once circled the office carrying three blank yellow legal pads for four straight hours, just to see if it could be done. No one batted an eye.

4: Avoid Eye Contact

The majority of serial killers/rapists will tell you that people don't remember what they looked like or even seeing them at all because they never made eye contact with anyone. So in order to slack off and take a nap or play a few extra hours of Leisure Suit Larry on the company dime, don't be afraid to borrow a page from the rapist/serial killer playbook. Just don't borrow the page about raping or serial killing. HR would have issues with that.

Sounds like a lot of work, doesn't it? Well, in a way it is. In fact, I'm sure there are days that I exert far more energy avoiding work than I would if I were simply to execute my mindless job. But it's a matter of principle, damn it.

Now if you'll excuse me, I have to carry this unopened package of printing paper upstairs to the Sales department, and then I have to bring it back here to my desk.

Five Ways to Avoid Being Given More Work at Your Office

The first time you are assigned an important project, wait until the deadline and then turn in a manila envelope filled with coleslaw.

While your boss is at lunch, move all of your stuff into his office and all of his stuff into your cubicle.

Tell your boss that you refuse to work on a project with people not of your race.

Wear a Lazer Tag vest around the office. Whenever your boss addresses you, drop to the ground and army-crawl behind the copier.

Wear an air horn around your neck. Whenever someone starts to assign you additional work, blow it in her face while maintaining steady, unflinching eye contact.

I Know What Really Goes On in These Cubicles

Before we begin, I just want to thank you for taking this time out of your busy schedule, Glen. I always look forward to doing my annual performance review with you.

I brought a copy of last year's performance goals and a spreadsheet showing how I met those goals. As you can see, my first goal was to have the best attendance in the office, which I achieved. I only missed the two half days when I was at my orthodontist.

I know on your spreadsheet it says Cassandra's attendance was the best, but that's wrong. She told Karen she was taking a personal day, but then she told you she was sick so it would count as a sick day instead of a personal day. If you don't believe me, here's a printout of the IM log I got off her computer.

I know we're not supposed to use the computers here for personal Internet use. So that's why I thought I'd bring that up. Even though Karen keeps checking vacation prices on Orbitz.com. And Brad looked at a Web site that had girls in bikinis on it. It's still in his Internet cache. No, it wasn't a sex site, it was just a sports site, but I still think it creates a hostile working environment.

Did you know Karen keeps selling chocolate bars for her daughter at work, even though we have a "no soliciting" policy in our company manual, on page 14? Right here. I highlighted it. I would never do that. Of course, I don't have children, but if God provides me with a husband someday and blesses me with children, I still would never cheapen that miracle by violating company policy.

My second goal was to effectively manage the switch to our new insurance provider. Isn't it amazing how much the company saves, just by making the office smoke-free and implementing a four-thousand-dollar annual deductible? Of course, Laura still smokes on her breaks. She goes out to the gazebo, where she thinks nobody can see her. But you know who can still see her? Lung cancer.

It's probably for the best that Laura had that abortion. Otherwise the kid would probably have lung cancer too. How do I know Laura had an abortion? Well, a little birdie told me. Actually, the birdie left a printout in our fax machine.

Laura was faxing her medical records to her new OB-GYN in July. But the first time it didn't go through. I have a copy of the error report if you'd like to see. I figured you had a right to know. I know this is a Christian office.

My final goal was to minimize office downtime. And our office birthday party celebrations are 71 percent more efficient now that we consolidate birthday parties to the third Friday of the month. It wasn't easy. Prakesh wouldn't tell anybody his birthday. But I got the month by looking at his license plate to see his renewal sticker, and then I got his birthday online. Then I did a little more Googling. Prakesh has a brother who is a registered sex offender. Did you know that?

The girl who refills our candy machines is a lesbian. I saw the rainbow flag on her car. Rainbow means gay.

No, that wasn't related to performance goals. I was just making small talk.

I Should've Been a Drug Dealer

Oh, sweet, my new keyboard came in. I was so tired of that "G" sticking on the old one. This just made my day!

Oh, shit. This new keyboard just made my day.

What the hell have I become? Is my life so empty that the arrival of a fifteen-dollar keyboard is the highlight of my week? This nine-to-five is really getting to me. This was supposed to be my way out of the ghetto, but these days I feel more trapped than ever. Shit, man, I should have just been a drug dealer.

Now, I've never been in a gang before, and neither have I ever engaged in the illegal sale of drugs, but how hard could it be? I got a cousin who's a drug dealer, and he's only a couple of IQ points above being legally retarded. However, he rolls a different car every week and constantly has a pocketful of Benjamins. Sure, he's been shot at, but he hasn't been hit yet, and on top of all that he gets laid like a modern-day Tupac. Now I ask you, who is the retarded one?

Besides, what good has this white-collar career done me? I'm called a sellout when I go back to the old neighborhood, and when I tell my coworkers where I grew up they get all freaked out and distant. I have a shitty studio apartment in an average neighborhood and I haven't gotten a raise of more than 3 percent since I got out of college. That's some fucked-up shit.

Now, if I had been a drug dealer I would be independently wealthy and respected by all, and I'd be the one calling the shots. I'd get up late and go to bed later. I'd call women "bitch" and "ho" instead of "miss" and "missus." Anyone who questioned my authority would think twice before doing it again, and despite my current stance on gun control I'd be packing some serious heat.

If it hadn't been for my tenth grade history teacher taking a special interest in me, I might be living this dream right now, but no, she had to "save me from the streets" and "steer me in the right direction." Is this the right direction, bitch? Middle-aged, single, and overwhelmingly depressed? Fuck this shit.

See, the problem is, it's too damn late to start now. While my sales and marketing skills got the potential to revolutionize the industry of illegal drug sales, my lack of street cred is likely to stand in the way of such a career change. Plus, it ain't like they got headhunters that can place you in a gig like that.

Fuck it. My fate's all sealed up and shit. I'm destined to live a life of mother-fuckin' mediocrity and unfulfilled desire like all the other bitches up in this of-fice. I had my chance and I blew it. If you ax me, I guess there's a reason my way is the road less traveled. That reason is, this fuckin' road sucks.

Now if you'll excuse me, I have a meeting with my cracker-ass supervisor. He'll prolly be complainin' at me about the way I'm doing my job and shit. He's one lucky motherfucker—if I was a dope man I'd have him taken out for sure.

Thank You for Attending This Suggestion-Box Meeting

Greetings, employees and temporary staff. Thank you all for your gracious attendance at this mandatory company meeting.

As many of you know, there is an employee suggestion box located on the wall just outside the kitchen. Most of you have the good sense to ignore it, but some of you feel the need to occasionally share your various petty gripes and hang-ups with those of us in upper management.

Anyhoo, HR encourages us to periodically have a meeting in which we publicly feign interest in and concern over your suggestions. We do this in order to make you all feel that you are valued and that your opinions are relevant. This is just such a meeting.

Upon my request, a list of your suggestions has been compiled by my secretary, Shari. Or Carrie. It's either Shari or Carrie. Something "arie." I don't know. She's only been here a few months.

Anyway, the following were your suggestions, in no particular order:

Employees using the microwave in the break room should be mindful of what they are cooking and shouldn't be heating up any of that funky Indian shit that Shibu is always bringing around.

Could whoever is leaving *Entertainment Weekly* in one of the bathroom stalls stop drawing boobs on Tom Cruise? You might not agree with his behavior or personal views, but he has still produced an impressive body of work that deserves more respect than you are giving him.

Melanie should go out with Jason. He has asked nicely more than a few times. The least she could do is have a drink with him. He doesn't bite.

Employees riding a bicycle to work should refrain from dragging it into the office and carrying it around like they are Captain friggin' Planet. We get it, Josh. You like the environment.

I don't think it's fair that black and Jewish employees get days off on their special holidays like Kwanzaa and Yom Kippur and still don't have to work on real holidays like Christmas and Easter.

Employees who are bilingual should not engage in Spanish conversations with the cleaning staff. We know that you guys are talking about us. We're not idiots.

The elevator in the West Building is for emergency use only. This is only a two-story building, and a few trips up the old steps aren't going to kill your fat ass, Mary.

Employees should refer to the company's employee handbook in regard to what is defined as "business casual," because apparently Renee Morley thinks it means "Go ahead and dress like a cheap prostitute."

Gambling is illegal and not permitted in any form at the office. That being said, Dave, let's just have one Super Bowl pool. No one is interested in your sixteen-tiered jack-off sweepstakes that you run every year.

I still don't see why employees can't use wood paneling that we bring from home to add makeshift ceilings to our workspaces, thereby instantly transforming them from "cubicles" into "little offices."

Melanie could at least respond to Jason's e-mails. The reason that he sends her all those funny forwards is because he thinks that the sound of her laughter is the most beautiful noise in the world. She probably doesn't even open them.

John can stop sending people links to things he has for sale on eBay. No one is even interested when you talk about your collection of antique lunch boxes, so why on earth would anyone want to buy them?

Though we recognize that participation on the company's softball team is "just for fun," could we please have a very basic tryout to make sure that players at least have minimal hand-eye coordination skills? This would ensure that they won't publicly shame our company with their complete lack of athletic ability. Or we could just lie to Jerry and tell him we're not having a team this year.

Speaking on behalf of all parents in the office, I would like to request that you force Russ Stack to take a mandatory sick day on this year's Bring Your Daughter to Work Day. I realize that his court case is still pending and that he has not yet been officially convicted, but an ounce of prevention is worth a pound of cure.

Anyhoo, I guess that's about it. I've read all of them aloud, with the exception of the inevitable few that described in great and colorful detail proposals concerning where on my person I could shove the suggestion box and in what manner I could accomplish these feats. But I won't be dignifying those with oration.

I hope you're all appeased for the time being. And if not, perhaps I'll have Shari/Carrie order you all a big ice cream cake or something. Carry on.

Oh, a New Screensaver. And It's Free!

Click on the pirate for a prize? Arrr! I'll get your treasure, pirate! Got him! Let's see what I won.

Oh, a new screensaver! And it's free!

For the life of me I don't know how they can afford to do this, just giving out free screen-savers willy-nilly. Who are these beautiful al-truists of cyberspace who take joy in such selfless acts of charity?

Hmmm. My computer's running kind of slow now . . .

Oh, hey, Dave? Dave! Over here. Sorry to bother you on your way back to your office, but I'm having some troubles with my com-puter and you're so good with this stuff. No, I didn't reinstall WeatherBug. My computer is just running really slow today, and I can't figure out why.

Okay, Tools, Options, and—yes, they're all enabled. I know last week you had me disable JavaScript and Flash, but I had to turn them back on to see the kitty. The kitty screensaver I won today. See? When you move your mouse over his paw, he reaches out like he wants that ball of string! Awwwww!

Sometimes the kitty is a little slow getting the string. He'll unfreeze in a minute. H*aaaaa*ng on. No, Dave, hang on, don't wander away. You're going to want to see this. Okay. T*aaaaaaaaaaa*kes a sec. Can't really do anything else with the computer while the kitty is in midswat . . . so, it's been a mild winter so far, huh?

Well, if you want to end the process, go ahead. Here, take the keyboard. Three keys at once is two keys too many for me. I'm lucky you stopped by. I don't see you so much, now that you take the long way to and from the men's room.

Here we go. Hey, what's that one called "PORNMONG.EXE"? Right under "WETHRBUG.EXE"? Oh. But how, exactly, do they turn my office computer into a pornographic spam remailer? Bad kitty! Bad kitty!

I wouldn't try uninstalling it if I were you. I tried to do that yesterday and up popped a cartoon in Russian. I couldn't understand it all, but apparently if I try uninstalling it again the guys who wrote it are going to find me and cut off my hands.

Quit judging me, Dave! I don't come by your office and tell you not to click on pirates!

Sure, run it if you think it will help. It gets rid of spyware, huh? Wow. I feel like double-oh-seven. Dum dum-dum-dum, dum, dum-dum-dum . . . Thanks, Dave. It won't happen again. Have a good one.

What's this? "Who's sexier, Paris Hilton or Angelina Jolie? Click one." Well, that's no contest—Angelina is a vision. I don't think I could live with myself if I didn't put in my two cents on this topic. (Click.)

Chapter Seven

Hey, Guys, What About Me?

Dear Myself in 1988

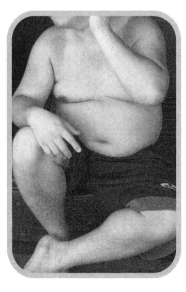

Dear Myself in 1988,

First of all, stop eating. Just because you can fit thirty Chicken McNuggets, two cheeseburgers, a large fries, and a chocolate milk shake in your stomach, it doesn't mean you should. You are going to want to have sex with a girl in the near future. They do not want to have sex with a kid with cake frosting spread across his chin and a belly hanging over his neon green Skidz. Knock it the fuck off and join a sports team. No, not fencing, you dickless pansy.

Okay, on to bigger and better things. You know that thing in the bathroom that hangs above the sink? It's called a mirror. It actually reflects images of things that are in front of it. Yup, that's you, the guy with the risky hair combination of spiked top and waterfall mullet. I don't get it. Why do you go to so much trouble just to look like an asshole? Why not just let your hair grow and just never comb it? You can give the same impression to people and not keep the Best Cuts at the mall in business for another week. Just because Bryan Bosworth does it doesn't mean it's sweet. I don't see you running to go get your face ripped off by Bo Jackson. Are you aware of the amount of times that you are within an arm's reach of scissors during any given day? You are in fifth grade, for Christ's sake. Your teacher has a bin full of them by the popsicle stick basket. Cut that shit off and start beating up some of the wimpy kids at lunch. This is the easiest time to acquire a tough-kid reputation by picking on the lower end of the food chain. Stop coloring pictures and drawing comic books. That shit is not going to work out.

The Buckeyes are going to go undefeated and win the national title in 2002. I'll send you a copy of the season results so you can accumulate a fortune. Don't fuck up and lose it, or I'm going to find a DeLorean with a flux capacitor and beat your fat little ass into the ground, which would essentially be me whipping my own ass. I would have so much more trust in you if you weren't me.

After the spike-haired mullet is done away with and your future is secure, go to your closet. Why do you only own ten pairs of neon-colored sweatpants? This is not the WWF—which is actually the WWE, but we won't get into that right now. Stop being a dipshit. Buy a pair of jeans that aren't black or acid-washed and put on a shirt that doesn't say HOBIE. This is probably the only generation in which you would get away with such a retarded image. In my time, people who dress the way you do are known as "shitheads." Shitheads *are known to frequent bowling alleys and trailer parks. They typically give a "thumbs-up" and a nod to anything remotely pleasant that's blurted their way. Take off the Pizza Hut sunglasses and stop humming while you walk. Watch some John Hughes movies and act cool like Judd Nelson. Girls do not think it is cool when you dress up like Freddy Krueger at recess. Why do I have to explain this shit to you? Damn it!*

There is so much more to say, but just work on the things I've informed you about here. Oh, yeah, take your Sega Master System and throw it against the wall. Save your allowance, admit you were wrong, and buy a Nintendo. Alex Kidd sucks ass and would turn tricks for Mario if Luigi would let him. Way to pick a moment to be an individual and fight the status quo. Now get outside, do something masculine, and stop being such a bitch.

Yourself,
Me

P.S. In 2002, don't draft Kurt Warner for your fantasy keeper league.

Sly's Not the Only Stallone Who Kicks Ass

Thank you, everybody, for coming tonight to share this special day with us. This is very exciting. Just in case anyone here doesn't know me, I'm Frank, and I want to say once again how honored I am to have been asked by Sly to be his best man here tonight. I know that he could have picked just about anyone to be up here right now. He's got some pretty high-rolling Hollywood friends. Kurt Russell, Chazz Palminteri, and Ray Liotta, just to name a few. But he asked me. So he was obviously going for family loyalty rather than star power.

Wait, why are you all laughing? That wasn't supposed to be some cute self-deprecating best man icebreaker joke. I'm being dead serious here, people. And I have a few things I've been wanting to say to this big lug for a long time . . .

You think you're cool, don't you? You think you're better than me. You sit there with that stupid crooked grin on your face, thinking you're the best thing since Mom's linguini alfredo. I know what he's thinking, ladies and gentleman.

"I'm Sylvester. My new bride is a hot piece of nineteen-year-old ass. I'm successful, I'm attractive, I take my shirt off in front of people, and I have a catalog of films the entire world will enjoy for years to come."

Well, those happen to be the only differences between us. Well, actually that's not true. There is one major difference that I neglected to mention. Sylvester pulls in about seven figures for doing a film, whereas I am lucky to get three. Let me talk, Grandma!

But other than that, Sly and I are almost exactly alike. We have the same last name, we're both very competitive, and we both live in his house. He's got that "thing" against Schwarzenegger and I have one against Eric Roberts, Julia's brother. If I play a down-and-out cop in Chinatown, then that son of a bitch follows up with the same thing. It gets frustrating after a while. I'm also competing against Joe Estevez, Daniel Baldwin, Don Swayze, Charlie Murphy, Jim Belushi, and Ashlee Simpson. Ashlee doesn't know it's happening, though.

Hey, can I get another Beam and Coke up here? What?! No, *you're* cut off!

You know, I could make thousands and thousands of dollars per film, but no one knows my movies exist. This business is all about marketing, people. The world would love *Outlaw Force* and *Lethal Cowboy* if anyone watched them. The same goes with *Total Force* and *Lethal Games*. There is a scene in *Lethal Games* that would kick ANY *Rocky* scene's dick in! Now *that's* a sweet-ass flick. We had a premiere and everything. Unfortunately, we couldn't get our projector to work, so we acted the whole thing out for the crowd. It really lost something in the translation.

Hey, does anyone remember *Copland*? What a fuckin' turd! What really pissed me off was that Sylvester put on a couple pounds for that role and he was the talk of Tinseltown. Meanwhile, I gained fifty pounds for *Easy Kill* and kept it on for my next six films and no one gave a shit. Then I packed on another thirty for the remainder of my career up till now. Still not one Oscar nod! It's all about who you know, people . . . who you know.

Okay, one quick side note: before I forget, I'd like to give a big fuck-you to my parents for naming me Frank. You couldn't have set me up for mediocrity any better than you did. You should have just gone ahead and named me Fail!

All right, let's raise our glasses . . . To my beloved brother and his new Lolita, who, fortunately for him, was only two when *Over the Top* came out, and therefore has probably never seen it. Sylvester, you're a fucking dick. May you and your hot little trophy wife burn in hell for eternity while watching *Rhinestone* and eating Planet Hollywood's shitty food. Cheers!

Man, Do I Love Stealing Your Music

Hey, popular recording artists, do you have a minute? Mr. Springsteen? Ms. Stefani? Mr. Diddy? Can I borrow you over here for just a sec? I know you're all very busy, but I wanted to let you know that I am simply nuts about stealing your music online.

Now, I recognize that many of you devote long hours to writing, recording, and producing your art. And I also understand that you feel that you should be fairly compensated for the fruits of your labor. But can I just say that I have an absolute blast thieving your life's work in minutes and listening to it at no cost? It's a gas!

And I don't just steal one or two songs, mind you, I snag your entire albums. As you know, oftentimes in the past buying a whole CD could be a real risk. You may have heard a catchy single on the radio and said, "Man, this Jet song is pretty good—I think I'll buy that disc." Only to get it home and find out that "Are You Gonna Be My Girl?" is the only listenable track on the whole album. Well, no more. Now I can pilfer your CD in its entirety and simply drag whatever portions of your precious work that don't meet my standards into the trash. Then I just flush them away into cyber nothingness with a click of my mouse. Flush! It's a fantastic process, and it's gotten so much easier. I used to have dial-up Internet, and back then it would take me a good ten minutes to steal your songs. But since my switch to DSL, I can snag the tune that took you months to conceive, write, and record in just under a minute. Boo-yah!

I've noticed that a lot of "pay" download sites have started popping up as a viable alternative to stealing music. And I commend this. The sites seem to be convenient, easily navigable, and inexpensive. Many downloads cost as little as one dollar. However, that being said, do you know what's even cheaper than one dollar? No dollars!

I probably wouldn't be as enthusiastic about horking your music if some of you weren't so darned whiny about it. "Stop stealing our music!" "It's not fair!" "I have a gardener to pay!"

Hey, Lars from Metallica. Get back behind your drums and quit crying. I don't even like your band that much because I've never owned a sleeveless black muscle shirt or sported a bad teenage mustache. But I still make it a point to steal all of your music just on principle. I've stolen every one of your albums, including the monstrously bad *Reload*, just to vex you. I don't even listen to them. I just buy a bunch of blank CDs, make hundreds of copies of all your albums, and then hand them out to people on the street for free. Keep those new tunes coming.

I know that you are all working hand in hand with the U.S. government right now to try to regulate this free-for-all and stamp out evil downloaders such as myself. And I wish you all the best of luck. But just remember that every time you find a way to shut down a Napster, a new site will pop up. Right now some wonderfully tragic geek in Germany with way too much time on his hands and no girlfriend is working around the clock to find a way around your new rules and antidownload technology. And he, my friends, is the real hero.

So in closing, fuck off, Oasis. And eat my ass, Ryan Adams. I own you. And you didn't cost me shit. Now if you'll excuse me, I hear good things about the new White Stripes album. Personally I think they're a bit overrated, but who cares? Don't cost nothin'!

Read My Blog!

Come on! I'm going to write something really insightful today. I promise! OMG! Yesterday I was on a roll when I wrote that fifteen-paragraph rant about my hatred for chocolate-covered peanuts. Just wait till you see me sound off on Rachel Lewis, the girl whose locker is next to mine. Oh, you're going to love it. I bet you can't wait to see what I have to say! You'll be ROTFLing!

Don't you wanna know why Maroon 5 is my favorite band? Don't you? I'll tell you why . . . in my blog, that is! I'll tell you my favorite songs and I'll list them in a kewl top-ten order. Then I'll talk about old-school rap and how hella kewl it is! In my blog!

My dog is the kewlest! His name is in my blog. You should read it! You'll know his name then and you can even see a picture of him at Halloween when I dressed him up as Jack White from the White Stripes. I was dressed up as Meg White. But you can see and read about all of this in my BLOG!!!

I wrote a poem for you in my blog. Just wait till you see what rhymes with Timberlake. I bet you can't guess. You should read my blog to find out. I totally have a crush on Mark Donovan in my sixth-period biology class. OMG OMG!!! Don't tell anyone. SHHHHHHhhhhh. I'll tell you more in my BLOG!!!

Oh, these problems I have with boys. Thank god I have a blog to talk to. You'll understand when you read my blog. If only some cute guys would read my blog. Then they'd see the real me and not the gaunt, rickets-ridden recluse that I appear to be. Oh, one day! When they read my blog! When YOU read my blog!

My stupid brother is playing his PlayStation in here now, so I have to go!!! But you can read more in my BLOG!!!!

L@@K in my BL@G!!!!

||||||||||||
L OO--\ K @ my blog!!!!!!!!
<|
~__|
LOL
ROTFL
BRB

By the Time You Read This, I'll Be Dead

By the time you read this, I'll be dead. Or maimed. Or maybe just napping. I'm really not sure. I'm kind of playing it by ear.

Don't get me wrong, I'm definitely going to kill myself. Crippling depression coupled with the sad realization that my life will never rise above the level of mediocre has solidified my decision to shed this earthly coil ASAP. But it seems like every time I try to end it all, something comes up.

I really meant to do it this past week, but I got pretty caught up in the NCAA tourney. But as soon as that wrapped up (Go, Florida!) I was ready to end this charade I call life. But suddenly *Superman 2* came on TNT.

Superman 2 is by far my favorite in the series. That's the one with General Zod and his two cohorts from Krypton. And plus, Lois finds out that Clark is Superman (duh). A lot of people prefer *Superman 3* with Richard Pryor, but that one's too jokey for me.

I haven't checked out the new *Superman* yet, but I heard they were originally talking about casting Nicolas Cage as the Man of Steel. What! Are you kidding me? Come on, Hollywood!

But anyway, I got really into that, and by the time the movie was over it was pretty late, so I decided to "do the deed" the next day.

So when I woke up that morning, I was like, "All right, Mike, it's go time," and I went downstairs to get a knife. But when I got to the kitchen I realized that I was pretty hungry and decided to grab a bite, because hey, even guys on death row get a last meal!

I remembered that I had a twenty-dollar gift certificate for the IHOP. I won it by calling in to Classic Rock 98.5 and answering the Lunchtime Drive-In trivia question, "What band first recorded the Paul McCartney–penned song 'Come and Get It'?" (Badfinger).

So I went down to the IHOP and PIGGED OUT! I figured, why not? No need to stick to the South Beach at this point! It was *soooooooo* good! (Me + strawberry-filled pancakes + butter pecan syrup = happy!) But as soon as I was done, I rushed home to end my life.

I got back to the kitchen, where, wouldn't you know it, there was not a clean knife in the place. They were all in the dishwasher, which had just finished its cycle and was waiting to be emptied. Now, my roommates and I have a little rule in our house. The first one to use a clean dish out of the dishwasher has to empty it. And I always end up getting stuck doing it! Nate and Chad would just let it sit there forever if they had their way. And I have a sneaking suspicion that they frequently use a clean dish and then just lock it back up and wait for The Sucker (me) to empty it.

Well, I refused to have my last act on earth be emptying the dishwasher, so I decided to find another way to abandon my mortal vessel.

Then I remembered that famous people like to kill themselves by eating a bunch of pills. So I figured that might be kind of a cool way to go. I started scrounging around the house for some drugs. Unfortunately, all that I could track down were five Tylenol PM, four Imodium AD, and a handful of Sucrets. Not exactly what you would consider a lethal combo, but I figured I'd give it a shot anyway and I swallowed the whole gang.

As you probably guessed, the dose didn't kill me, but it did make me crap like a madman! I was on the pot for so long that I was too tired when I got off to even think about committing suicide. So I decided to finish myself off in the morning.

The next day, I planned to kill myself by parking my car in my garage and leaving the engine running, the way a young John Cusack tried to do it in the cult eighties movie *Better Off Dead*. Which still holds up as a pretty funny flick even though it's really dated. Check it out.

So I pulled the old Tempo into the garage and anticipated that the next voice I heard would be that of St. Peter, welcoming me to Paradise.

Instead it was my neighbor Steve, with whom we share a garage. He was doing some work on his fence and wanted to borrow my posthole digger. I told him that was fine and we both went back about our business. Unfortunately, Steve was in and out of the garage so much getting tools that the carbon monoxide kept escaping. So after six hours, not only was I not dead, I was low on gas and had a killer headache. I went back inside, cheated by life once again. I went to bed with my head pounding and no relief in sight, as I had taken all the Tylenol PM the night before. (When it rains, it pours!)

So here I am now. Poised to leap off the Rocky River Metropark Bridge. Ready to plummet into the sweet abyss that is eternity. But you know, now that I really look at it, this might not be high enough of a jump to kill me.

I had thought about driving to the Independence Overpass Bridge. Now that baby's high! That definitely would have done it. But it's kind of far and I would have had to stop to get gas. (Two-ninety-one a gallon—F that!)

I just called down to some kids who were fishing below me, and they answered. That probably means I'm not high enough.

Oh, elusive Grim Specter of Death, when will you finally harvest this wayward soul?

It's cold up here. I think I'll mosey home and watch some E! network.

Why Am I Such a Lard-Ass?

Do these panties make my clit look fat? They totally do, don't they? No wonder Aaron left me for that bitch Hilary Duff. My clit looks so fat and disgusting in these panties. I can see the headlines now: "Lindsay Lohan Has a Gross, Fat Clit!"

Oh, who am I kidding? It's not the panties that make my clit look fat. My clit is fat. I hate it so much. I mean, look at it! I finally got rid of my huge tits and my luscious ass, and now this. I'm so ugly and worthless.

Wilmer used to tell me that I had a beautiful clit and that I shouldn't worry about it. Like I'm gonna take advice from the guy who plays Fez. Puh-leez! If Kelso told me that my clit wasn't fat, I might believe him. But Ashton wouldn't even look twice at a clit this big unless he was trying to punk me or something. God, I'm such a tub of lard. My love bug is fully loaded . . . with fat.

I've got no one to blame but myself. I ate like a whole bag of baby carrots yesterday. Everyone knows that carrots go straight to your clit. I don't know what I was thinking. I might as well just call it a cock and be done with it. Maybe if I throw up a little more I can bring it down to size. I need some coke.

I wish I was more like Paris Hilton. Her body is so perfect. She's so in shape that she doesn't even get a period anymore, much less have to worry about her clit bulging out of her panties. Why can't my clit be like that? I wish I had never been born.

I heard a rumor that Paris went to this Saudi doctor out in Van Nuys who actually knows how to remove clits. He's really more of a barber, but I hear that's pretty much the same thing over there, so it's, like, totally safe. Plus, I guess it's like some kind of Islamic custom or something, which is cool. I wonder if that's, like, the same as Kabbalah? I hear all the girls in Arabia and Africa get their clits removed when they turn twelve. They are so lucky! Must be nice. Why don't they do that here? I hate America. I hate my clit. I hate myself.

Help Me, Star Jones—You're My Only Hope

Oh, come on. Not now. Now is really not a good time for a hard-on. Yeah, I know I'm sixteen years old and I pitch a tent twenty times a day for no particular reason, but we're in the middle of my little brother's bar mitzvah here. I'm about to have go up on stage for a family picture with the fucking rabbi! I don't need all of Temple Beth Shalom checking out my wood.

Damn it. I should've seen this coming. I didn't get to jerk off last night because I had two of my cousins sleeping on cots in my room. If either of those sneaky bastards had heard me jacking it, the whole family would've known by sunrise. And when you add that the little sluts in my brother's Hebrew school class wear some skimpy-ass shit in the House of the Lord, it's no wonder I'm at Def Cock 5.

Okay, come on. Think. What usually works? Grandma. Of course. Floppy skin, blue hair, eau de mothballs, and the fact that Dad sprang out of her beaver in 1957. She's a guaranteed chubbie deflater. But wait. Oh, man, she's sitting like five feet away, and—oh, shit—she just smiled at me! While I was in the middle of thinking how disgusting she would be in just her girdle! Oh God, this is so wrong. Abort! Abort!

All right, forget Grandma. Let's try something else. Okay, how about baseball? That's supposed to work too, right? Okay, picking dirt from my cleats, sweaty batting gloves, Randy Johnson's pockmarked face (and that mullet he used to have back in Seattle), a big wad of tobacco that looks like a dog turd protruding from Manny's mouth as he steps up to the plate. Yes, yes, it's working. I'm starting to soften up. Okay, what else? That fat kid on my Babe Ruth league team whose jersey was way too small. Yeah, yeah, that was fucking sick. This boner doesn't stand a chance!

Oh, no, wait a minute. Didn't that fat kid sit next to me when our team had that end-of-the-season trip to Yankee Stadium? That was the game where that girl in the cutoff Jeter T-shirt sat in front of us. Oh, shit. She was totally nipping out when she walked down the row to her seat. And then there was that panty shot we got when she sat down. They were pink with lace trim and they were shouting "Me so horny!" the entire game and—God dammit—Mr. Stiffie is back up in it! Son of a bitch!

Anyway, fuck! The photographer is getting into position and the rabbi is motioning to us to come up on stage and I'm still sitting here with a pup tent. I need a serious miracle here. I gotta get rid of this fucking thing in like fifteen seconds.

Okay, I'll take anything. What's in my field of vision? Windows, carpet, flowers, Star of David, some bald guy . . . Wait, that's it! Star. Star Jones!!

. . . Hard-on reducing! Yes! It's working. Total deflation has been achived.

Thank you, Star Jones! You banished my boner and got me ready for the camera. Thank you from the bottom of my heart, you magnificently repulsive warthog.

The Five Worst Times to Get Wood

5. While riding on the back of a guy's motorcycle

4. While singing in a barbershop quartet

3. Just before you give your final summation in a murder trial

2. While dancing with the bride

1. When you're holding a baby

I Am My Car

I am a Cadillac Deville. This baby was $42K, and that comes with a deed to the road. You get what you pay for, and what I paid for was the right to drive here in the left lane at 59 mph. What I paid for was the right to turn left from the right lane, because I have someplace to be and a Caddy to take me there. I've got 2,400 pounds of Detroit steel, and sometimes that steel misses its exit. I don't have to go to the next exit and turn around . . . they put reverse in this car for a reason. Get out of my way, because I am my car.

I am a 2006 Corvette. I am hot, sexy, and fifty-three years old. I am balding, but I have a baseball cap on so you can't tell. I used to have a wife and two kids, but now I have a "hot" forty-two-year-old girlfriend with implants that aren't fooling anyone, alimony and child support payments, a car insurance bill that could feed all of a small South American country, and an efficiency apartment. And I have a 2006 Corvette. I am a bad-ass, because I am my car.

I am a Hummer H2. I am gigantic. My penis is small, but my car is HUGE. I can run over your Civic on the way to the gas station, again. I could definitely go off-road in the desert or something, but I might ruin the paint job. I just ran over your three-year-old in my driveway because I couldn't see him. I am huge. I am my car.

I am a Volkswagen Cabriolet, but I call it my "Cab." I am adorable, I am twenty-two, and I am in the business sorority. Daddy bought me this car, and it is the cutest thing EVER. I see you looking at me as you drive by, and I just stare aloofly forward, refusing to even acknowledge your existence if you don't have a Beamer or a Wrangler. I am priceless. I am my car.

I am a RAV4. I used to drive a Cab in college, but now I need to take the kids to ice skating practice. I'm still cute. I am! Dammit! Look at me! You, in the Beamer! You tight little twenty-three-year-old in the Wrangler! I'm still cute! I am my car!

I am a Jeep Wrangler. I am blaring Dave Matthews. I am wearing a backward baseball cap that says "South Carolina COCKS." I have flip-flops on in January. My collar is popped. I am wondering why that scary-looking woman in the RAV4 is yelling. I am going to get laid tonight, because that's what I do. I am my car.

I am a 1978 Cutlass Supreme. My back window is held on with duct tape. I used to have a rear bumper. My left front door is a different color from the rest of the body. Only one of my headlights works, but I can see fine because of the sparks from my dragging muffler. I so don't give a shit about this car. I don't need to look when I change lanes. Does it look like I have anything to lose? I dare someone to hit me. I am my car.

I am a minivan. I am a dad. I used to be a 300Z. I loved that 300Z. I can handle this thing as if it were a 300Z. I can weave in and out of traffic. I have sport striping, dammit! I am a cool dad! Maybe I'll just trade the whole damn package—minivan, wife, kids—in for a Corvette and that tramp bartender from Billy's Place. But for now, I am my car.

I am an Audi A3. I am going to Slide, or Fly, or some other one-word-verb-named club to drink expensive martinis and fuck hot rich chicks. I will tell you not to scratch the paint, valet. I am my car.

I am a Toyota Corolla. I just got out of college, the one named on the sticker on the back window. I have a good job. I am dependable. I am boring. I am my car.

I am a Hyundai Elantra. I just graduated from the community college in the back window. I will tell anyone who will listen that my car was three grand cheaper than a Toyota and has a ten-year, 100,000-mile warranty. I won't believe a word I'm saying. I wish I had a Toyota. I am my car.

I am a panel truck. Observe my ladders strapped to every surface, though not terribly well. My ride is piled high with boxes, furniture, a couple animals, and some immigrants. Any one of these things may come flying off at any time. Do not follow closer than half a mile. I am my car.

You Can't Plinko for Shit, You Dumb Bitch

Are you retarded, lady? Because if so, I'll give you a pass. But anything short of Down's would officially make you the worst Plinko player in the history of *The Price Is Right*! And this show has been on since World War I. Bob Barker started it in 1917 as a patriotic service to keep war brides distracted from the bloodshed raging on the western front. *TPIR* has been rolling ever since.

And in all that time, never has there been a Plinko contestant who has rivaled you in sheer impotence and stupidity.

Just look at yourself. You have one god-damned Plinko chip. And that's the free one that Mr. Barker, in his unfailingly magnanimous nature, saw fit to GIVE you, despite that you guessed NONE of the prices correctly on any of the four common, everyday grocery items that were presented before you.

Speaking of which, I have a question for you, a nagging little query that I couldn't help but reflect upon throughout your truly atrocious Plinko performance thus far: Have you ever actually entered a grocery store in your entire life? And are you familiar with the commerce system that has been established here in the United States, in which goods are exchanged for monetary compensation? If so, are you aware that the amount of money exchanged for said items—the "price," if you will—remains fairly consistent throughout the country at any given time?

I am forced to assume that you are not. What other reason could there possibly be for you to guess that a twenty-two-ounce bottle of Selsun Blue Shampoo would cost $11.99 rather than $5.99?

Have you never purchased a bottle of shampoo? Do you go through life with unclean hair? Or do you make your own shampoo at home with spices and herbs from your garden?

Imbecile!

And are you honestly going to tell me that you are of the belief that you can get a box of Quaker Oats Instant Oatmeal for $1.99 rather than $3.99? It was a variety pack of four different flavors, bitch! Eight individual pouches! What kind of dream world are you living in where you can get a quality oatmeal product like that for two bucks? Because I want to start shopping there.

So now there you stand, atop the historic Plinko board, looking over the precipice of morning game show destiny, clinging to your one, sad, unearned Plinko chip. And you're debating where to drop it. Right now you have it poised directly above the $10,000 spot, as if the fucking thing is going to drop straight down.

Now, even if you have never seen this game before, surely you must have at least a loose grasp of general physics and the concept of gravity. Do you not think it might hit a couple of those spokes on the way down? Don't you think that might disrupt the trajectory of the chip a bit?

Jesus!

As if I didn't have a hard enough time watching the Cliff Hanger game today. That stupid marine couldn't price his way out of a paper bag. And it was with great pleasure that I watched the yodeling mountain climber plummet off the cliff, robbing Private Inbred of that handsome home entertainment package that included a La-Z-Boy recliner, a Panasonic plasma-screen TV, and a Jolly Time old-fashioned popcorn machine—"Jolly Time: Something Good Is Popping Up."

And now I'm subjected to this wretched Plinko display. And do you know what the worst part is? Regardless of your miserable showing, you still get to spin the

Rejected pricing game #02461

Prize Wheel. Simply because you won your way on stage by bidding one dollar on that ProForm treadmill. And you bid that only because the audience screamed it at you incessantly. You probably didn't even know what you were saying. You were just repeating a sound you heard like some witless mynah bird.

And because the Prize Wheel involves no skill or intelligence whatsoever, you might even end up in the Showcase Showdown. Of course, that's assuming you can grasp that you are supposed to spin the wheel, and you don't try to eat it or bang your head on it: two scenarios I consider alarmingly possible. Rod Roddy would roll over in his rhinestone-encrusted casket.

It would almost be worth it to see you get to the Showdown, though. The result could be highly entertaining. Seeing as how you were baffled when forced to decide whether a box of Crispix cereal was $4.99 or $8.99, it would be sadistically fun to watch your mind reel as you tried to tally the cumulative worth of a set of golf clubs, a trip to Portugal, and a dune buggy. You'd probably get really confused and end up bidding "hot dog."

Rejected pricing game #31604

So you've finally decided to drop your lone Plinko chip, at Bob Barker's kind but firm insistence. You watch painfully as it ricochets around briefly and then lands in the $0 slot.

Bob feigns compassion, but we all know he was rooting against you too. The morons that he has endured during his impressive tenure on this show must eventually wear on his patience. I'm sure he would agree with me when I implore you to do society a service and ensure that you never reproduce. Have yourself spayed or neutered.

Having a Huge Penis Is Not So Great

We really have to put a stop to this glorification of giant penises. Seriously, I can't take it anymore. From pills like Longitude to Swedish penis pumps, the fascination with having a monster manhood is out of control. I'm going to let you in on a little secret. I happen to have one of those "huge cocks," and it isn't all it's cracked up to be.

Yeah, yeah, I suppose it's better than having a really small penis, but this damn thing hanging between my legs is ridiculous. If I had the option, I'd trade it in for regular-size member in a second. Shit, I'd even take one on the small side. Five inches sounds great to me. I'm not kidding. There are three inches of me that is still a virgin. That's just frustrating. There's only so many times you can hear, "Slow, slow, slow, ouch" before you start to wonder if it's all worth it.

Everybody always focuses on the few positives, but let me tell you, it ain't all church picnics and ice cream sandwiches. Most of the time it's just a nuisance.

Take for example your morning BM. I bet you don't even think about it when you roll out of bed, grab the *Daily Tribune*, and head for the head. Well, not me. No reading the newspaper while I cut turds. I need both hands—one to wipe and one to hold my stupid giant penis. One slipup and my junk is bobbing in the bowl with a school of bumpy brownfish. Sound like fun to you?

And I can't tell you how many times I've missed the first ten minutes of a movie because I'm getting the third degree from the damn ticket taker about trying to smuggle in outside food.

"Sir, you can't take that cappicola into the theater."

What am I supposed to say? There are kids around. It's embarrassing.

And how about shorts? Those must be nice. It's damn hot right now in Los Angeles, but unless I want to risk exposing myself to the world, I am in trousers. I can't even wear boxer shorts. You see, it's not just the size; it's the weight. I need some support. Not that briefs don't pose their own set of problems. Putting them on is like trying to stretch a twin-size fitted sheet over a king-size mattress, but it's better than the back problems I had when I was letting that monstrosity hang free.

Don't even get me started on condoms . . . Magnum, you say? Yeah, right. Those things are like a tourniquet. I might as well try to squeeze into a Ken doll's tuxedo.

Sure, there are some girls who love a great big penis, but those girls are all skanks. I'm looking for a nice girl, not some loose tramp who I am embarrassed to take home to my mom. And don't try to tell me you are a nice girl who likes her men big. If your G-spot is the underside of your left ventricle, you are a skanky ho, and I am not introducing you to my family.

Guys are even worse. In public restrooms I try to be discreet and pull out just enough to keep my pants dry, but there is always some guy staring at me. What

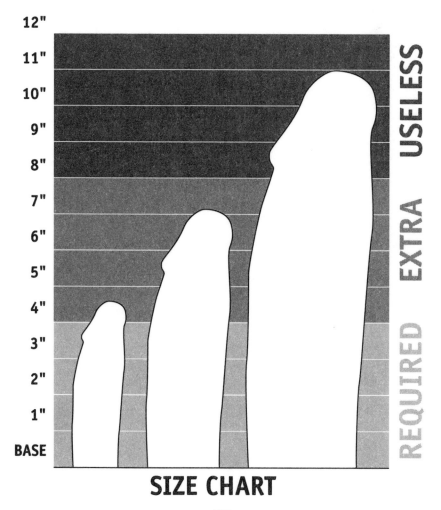

SIZE CHART

is the fascination? It's just a big penis, for God's sake. I don't want to hear about how "not gay" you are either; just look up and finish your business. And no, you cannot touch it, so stop asking me! I am a human being, not some freak-show petting zoo.

So the next time you see a well-hung porn star like Lexington Steele plowing some professional penis rider, remember that not all of us are porn stars. Some of us are just regular guys trying get through the day without closing our big, dumb penis in a car door. Be thankful you don't have to worry about that.

The Writers

Mike Polk Jr. is a marketing producer at the Cleveland CBS affiliate station. He is the author of the original article "Look at My Striped Shirt" and acted as The Phat Phree's editor for this book.

Look at My Striped Shirt!

I Am the Karaoke Master

I Don't Care for the Term "Door Guy"

My After-Hours Party Is Going to Rock

Seriously, Dude, Give Me My Keys

It's Ladybugs for Me!

Being a Cop Makes Me Important

Buy Something at My Shitty Garage Sale

I'm So Glad You Caught Me, Kid

This Gangbang Is So Awkward

Welcome to Every Date Ever

Darling, If You Really Loved Me, You'd Bleach Your Asshole

Can't You Just Get a Cab to the Abortion Clinic?

High School Football Is All I Have

I Have Amazing Taste in Music

These Personalized License Plates Should Get the Word Out That I'm a Huge Douchebag

Man, Do I Love Stealing Your Music

By the Time You Read This, I'll Be Dead

You Can't Plinko for Shit, You Dumb Bitch

He cowrote:

The World Is My Phone Booth!

I'm Just Like One of the Guys!

Turn Signals Are a Waste of My Time

Charlie DeMarco is the creator and editor of The Phat Phree. He is a comedy writer and Internet developer from Cleveland who now lives and works in Los Angeles.

I'm Going to Hook You Up with This Cell Phone, Bro

No, I Don't Feel Any Different

I'm Feeling Lucky Today

Damn, My Pencil-Thin Beard Is Perfect!

Having a Huge Penis Is Not So Great

Scott Hofman isn't very good at writing bios.

I'm Going to Run onto the Field

America Is for Americans

Pot Really Opens My Mind

I Should've Been a Drug Dealer

He cowrote:

I'm a Real Fan

Turn Signals Are a Waste of My Time

Alex Blagg is a writer and comedian living in New York City.

We're Just Like Sex and the City*!*

I WILL Get Off This Plane Before You

Cheer for Them and I Will Punch You

This Office Snack Situation Is Unacceptable

Michael Martone is a playwright and medical student. He lives in Chicago.

I Just Made Some Statements That I Can't Back Up

I'm, Like, Really into Philosophy

I Am Perfect for This Job

I Know What Really Goes On in These Cubicles

Oh, a New Screensaver. And It's Free!

Chad Zumock is a writer and stand-up comic living in Los Angeles.

I'm Your Bartender, and I Hate You

Nice to Meet You, Lying Whore

I Am So Naked in This Locker Room

I Love the Gym

Jim Fath is a Cleveland native and forever-cursed Browns fan who lives and works out of Chicago. He's been in and written some shows that you've never heard of, and he'd also like to thank some people you don't know.

I Am the Greatest Pretend Worker This Company Has

Thank You for Attending This Suggestion-Box Meeting

Read My Blog!

He cowrote:

The World Is My Phone Booth!

Patrick O'Connor is a political cartoonist and illustrator living in Los Angeles. He draws five editorial cartoons each week for the *Los Angeles Daily News*.

He did all the sweet illustrations in the book.

Aaron McBride is a Cleveland-based writer and a cast member of the sketch-comedy group Last Call Cleveland.

I'm Your Cool Teacher

Sly's Not the Only Stallone Who Kicks Ass

He cowrote:

Captain's Log: Stardate 3272. Kirk Rocks!

Jesse Lamovsky likes to refer to himself as a "typist," but in reality he is a full-time unpaid writer from Kent, Ohio. Jesse has long considered suicide but has put those plans on hold, pending a Cleveland championship.

This Sunoco Is Now Open

I Have a Request, Mr. DJ

M. Thomas L. is a full-time pedagogue at the Introvert Academy. He is currently being devoured by a series of misunderstood projects and a continuous jones for Zagnut bars.

This Hot Chick Bartender Wants Me

He cowrote:

I'm a Real Fan

Ryan McKee is a writer, comedian, and music-trivia nerd living in Los Angeles. He also likes Corn Nuts.

I'm Yelling Things from My Car!

This Week Is Going to Be Brutal

Mike Hagesfeld is a comedy writer, improviser, and actor from Cleveland who depends to a ridiculous degree on his wife, Elise.

RE: It's Great to Be Back!

I Am My Car

Rob Sanford is the pen name of a New York attorney whose paranoia and narcissism make him think that using his real name in this book could jeopardize his pathetic excuse for a legal career.

Why Must You Always Be So Negative?

Help Me, Star Jones—You're My Only Hope

Ben Lambert is a writer from Illinois. He enjoys short walks on the beach because of a painful heel spur.

No Substitutions, Y'all

Half of This Relationship Is Not Working

Justin Harvey is a music producer and comedy writer as well as being one of the partners in Phamily Business Entertainment, the parent company of The Phat Phree.

We Own This Battle of the Bands

Ron Babcock is a comedian and filmmaker from Scranton, Pa., which is famous for mining coal and depression. He now lives in Los Angeles.

You Bet You Can Take My Order

Steve Kiley writes, sells stuff, and fishes for striped bass in the summer with his big black rod.

I Want You to Be in My Wedding!

Brenda Della Casa is a mogul-in-training who is currently writing, acting, and casting in New York City. She and her Chihuahua, Tony Montana, are plotting to take over the world.

Does This Outfit Make Me Look Slutty Enough?

Chris Browne is a sales guy by day who spends his time talking about fun and exciting stuff like revenue streams and enterprise software solutions. He also tries to forget about all of this by writing comedy at night while drinking copious amounts of wine and other fine alcoholic beverages.

Hey, Man, Check Out My Script

Juan Turlington is a writer based in Cleveland. His restrictive occupation keeps him from revealing his true identity and background. While this annoys and angers him, it does make him feel somewhat like a superhero.

Dear Myself in 1988

Josh Bacott is the founder of JoeSportsfan.com.

Dear Chris Berman

Brandon Gnetz is a Nashville-based writer who writes things down sometimes.

My Eighth-Grade Dance: An Open Apology

The Writers

Jason Mathews lives and works in Chicago. He hopes to someday have his own episode of A&E's *Biography* instead of this shitty little bio. Hopefully they won't be able to run it during "Serial Killers" week.

Why Am I Such a Lard-Ass?

Jon Santos is a sweet writer and friend to all.

My Fantasy Football Team Is Unstoppable

Justin Wood works in market research in Minneapolis. He has an autographed photo with Dustin Diamond. Jealous?

Seriously, Get This Sweater Off Me

Jef Etters is a writer and musician from Akron, Ohio.

He cowrote:

Captain's Log: Stardate 3272. Kirk Rocks!

Jessica Joy Kemock did sketch comedy and improv in L.A., and now she does it in Chicago. No big whoop.

She cowrote:

I'm Just Like One of the Guys!